The Streets of Odeon

by Edward Payne

The Streets of Odeon

by Edward Payne

published by

Fanfare Books

Stratford, Ontario

The Streets of Odeon

Printed in Canada

Typeface: Garamond

Edited by John Lederman
Design and Layout by John Lederman and Bob Newland
Back cover and spine by Everett Newland

Library and Archives Canada Cataloguing in Publication

Payne, Edward, 1926-
The streets of Odeon / Edward Payne.

ISBN 0-9738565-5-6

1. Payne, Edward, 1926- . I. Title.

PS8631.A954Z477 2006 C818'.603 C2007-902639-7

Foreword

I mention in the book that I would rather be lucky than clever. The fact that this book (these books actually, there is a first volume) was/were put together and published at all is entirely due to being in the right place at the right time.

I sit in the park here in Stratford every summer and display and sell small watercolours to the tourists. One day two terribly nice people came through and were friendly and kind. They had just moved to town. In the conversation I asked them what they did.

"We are book publishers," they say.

I say, "I've written a book."

They say, "Love to read it."

Politeness, I think, but give them the whole mess, a rambling incoherent account of my luck in life, roughly from the thirties, when little, to now. They read it and loved it. The rest was easy for me.

They worked and worked and produced a nice looking, well-put-together little soft back book. I was so proud and it did quite well selling the first modest run. Then they encouraged and shepherded the second volume and here it is.

It is again a narrative of how I saw things and how I remember people and matters that impressed me at the time. There are no chapters, rather things that just happened, good and bad. I tried, throughout my life, to behave decently and to do the right thing.

I am fortunate to have married two wonderful, long-suffering women, Vianne and Mary. I salute you both. I would have been long gone by now if it hadn't been for your care and love. Bless you both, still very good and loving friends. To my daughter Vicky, whom I adore, we seem so much alike at times a female version of me, thank you.

Thank you to all the marvellous people who encouraged and helped me and told me when I was doubtful, that I could write, laughed at my silly stories and my absurdities: to Stacey and Stephen Newman, my first publishers who changed my life and whom I shall always love; to Bob Newland, my present publisher and advisor in this risky and sometimes frightening but exhilarating adventure; to Erika Schiller for all her help with distribution; to John Lederman, who edited from my original stream-of-consciousness writing and yet managed to retain my voice, then designed and generally put together what I think is a very attractive publication; to she-who-wishes-to-remain-anonymous who found things half a dozen of us previously missed (what remains that may be thought 'errors' are due to an impossible deadline and are quirks of style and decisions of others—not your fault); to Kelley Teahen for her wise advice about tone, voice, and narrative; to Tyler-Addison Collins for her glowing appraisal; to Christopher Plummer for his kind and generous words of encouragement; and to the many others in my life with whom I had the precious experiences to write about here, and to share now with others.

I hope you like it.

To Gordon Price who made me laugh.

To Jamie Sandilands who made me laugh and wonder.

To Lovell Payne who made me laugh, wonder and love.

Preface

The meaning of the title is indicative of the fact that, in effect, I was as much raised by the cinema as I was by my parents. How often did I hear Mum or Dad saying on a Saturday afternoon, "Here's a shilling. Go to the pictures."

So I saw life in the world of the past, the present, and the future as flickering black and white moving pictures. I was led to believe America would be all sun, surf, beautiful girls, well-stocked bars, and lavish cafés with a program of endless fun and games...

Advice From My Father:
Never run up to a horse or a woman;
Never take an umbrella to the country;
Never wear a russet suit to the city;
Always know when to leave...

Bob carried my bags inside. There were not many, as I had sent all my heavy stuff by sea, my books, some souvenirs from Africa, other stuff that one buys to show people who never seem as interested as you think they will be and which finish up in the garbage.

I sat with cup of coffee surrounded by family. It all felt vaguely unreal after so many years of being alone, to be suddenly connected again to relatives of such closeness, but closeness without the intimacy that comes with familiarity. My sister regarded me with an expression of pride and pleasure. Bob, who I had last seen at the pub in London at the wedding celebration in the middle of a buzz bomb attack, was huffing and puffing with hospitality and considerateness, thoughtfully refilling my cup, and giving me cigarettes, which, being filterless Americans, made me cough and choke, much to the amusement of the two children who were sitting at my feet gazing up at me with awe and, I thought, some apprehension. This puzzled me until later Bob told me that they hadn't believed I was who I said I was, but a spy.

I slept badly that night, over-tired, over-excited, and anxious about the future. God, I must have been mad giving up what might have been a future of some promise in Sudan for what turned out to be an empty, hopeless, non-existent future with Laura. My stomach fell with that sickening feeling one gets when feeling sorry for oneself in matters romantic. Full of foreboding, I fell into a troubled sleep.

Laura at Idlewild, New York

My mood was not improved next morning when waking up and looking out of the window to see enormous drifts of snow everywhere. It had snowed and blowed heavily during the night. I was going to have to get used to this, as Wisconsin was a northern state subject to frequent storms and was generally unpleasantly cold. After the hot years in Africa, I was going to have my hands full to adjust to this new challenge.

* * * *

Weeks and months passed. The main preoccupation was to find a job. I was to find it even harder here to find something that would satisfy me financially and keep and hold my interest. I realized that all the experience I had had as a sales engineer was of no importance without the academic and professional qualifications required in the engineering field in the U.S.A. I determined to look elsewhere for employment.

Advertising and public relations seemed to be the areas that might make use of the qualities I vaguely felt I possessed. I wasn't sure what these were, but drawing and illustration had always been a facility. I was fairly literate, had good manners, was quite erudite, knew which fork to use first, was a quick learner, and America was going through a period of loving everything English, especially in positions of dealing with matters of liaison. My Fair Lady had just opened on Broadway and, generally, I thought the world would be my oyster. But I was to suffer a few disappointments before the shell opened for me.

Copious letters of application were written, carefully composed résumés were prepared, discreetly modest, but with what I considered to be gentle and diffident allusions to educational excellence in varying departments of learning, not overdoing the academic tendencies, but explaining, as it were, the quality of the vessel that only needed to be filled with problems of a commercial nature, to find its place in the sun.

These pleas for attention were sent to all the ad agencies I could find plus companies like Schweppes. I had drunk enough of their tonic to make me a director. Of course, throughout all these efforts, I found the attractiveness of what I imagined the ad business to be like, utterly appealing, grey flannel suits, martinis on home-going trains, white station wagons and golf club memberships. But alas it was not to be. Though most companies answered my highly embellished applications, they all were in the form of polite expressions of disinterest.

Again, as in the past, I was to have to depend on luck putting me in the right place at the right time. It was to come, this time, in ecclesiastical form. One of my sister's friends, a local Catholic priest, had mentioned to her that he knew someone with lots of money who had started a small company of an electronic nature and who was looking for an assistant whose duties would include matters of design and publicity and who would have to travel extensively. Bingo. Where do I sign?

In short order contact was made and I was standing in what I thought was a relaxed but respectful manner in front of this remarkable man's desk. Mr. Merrill Saunders. He virtually leapt to his feet with a grace and alacrity belying his stature, which was, to say the least, expansive. He was tanned and impressive, greying and handsome. He wore an expensive-looking white linen suit and he shook my hand with a dry and strong hand. He 'welcomed me aboard' in a loud booming voice. This nautical allusion, I found out, was an affectation he had adopted having served on carriers in the Pacific during the war.

We sat and talked. He explained the product they were trying to develop and market, a paint that produced high heat when connected to an electric power source. 'Bizarre,' I thought. 'The whole process was in some flux' and I 'would be coming in on the ground floor,' he continued in a manner both affable and purposeful. I warmed to him and felt a strong surge of wanting to work with him and an even warmer feeling that he liked me and at the end of this day, I was to be employed. We sat and talked more. We drank gallons of coffee and Coke and smoked.

The room that was his office was in itself a place of interest and disheveled luxuriousness, hand-made furniture, thick rugs of modern abstract design, colourful posters on the walls, plants everywhere, a well-stocked bar, wicker and bamboo with sunlight bathing the whole with bright but diffused light.

There was a long pause. Merrill got up and strode across the room. He really was a big man. He opened the door and yelled, "Roscoe, come and meet my new assistant." OH THIS WAS FANTASTIC, THE JOB WAS MINE.

I met the yelled-at man, who turned out to be the inventor of this mysterious product, one Roscoe Verney. Here was another character. He was a scruffy-looking individual who was apparently, a genius with numerous patents under his belt, friendly in a distant absent-minded way, looking more like a farmer than an engineer. He had a hayseed, Will Rogers, down home kind of appearance with, I learned later, a cutting sense of humour and an impatient manner with most people and certainly did not suffer fools gladly.

We all went, after the introductions, to a bar near the office where I was introduced to "sipping whiskey." This was a heavy, slightly sweet and very intoxicating liquor called Jack Daniels, a prime bourbon usually drunk neat or with a little water, when it was called "bourbon and branch." We all got very tight as we all had empty stomachs, so we then roared off in Merrill's flashy convertible, which was in a startling livery of orange and cream and chrome 'I-was-in-heaven,' to a nearby roadhouse.

In those days there were no restrictions, or for that matter, disgrace, in driving and drinking. In retrospect I often wonder how we survived the sixties, hard liquor, heavy smoking, diets of meat, potatoes and gravy, no greens to speak of, rich desserts, and late nights, never mind the fast and alcoholic driving. At the restaurant we were plied with that sort of meal, excessive, abundant, and totally wonderful.

As we talked and laughed and ate, smoking and sipping between mouthfuls, Merrill's other interests were brought up. He loved to fly, and had, in fact, an aircraft on the company's books. He took every opportunity to use it and mentioned that we were to go to Chicago soon and that he expected me to accompany him. I kept thinking, money has not been mentioned yet, and I hated to bring it up and spoil all the bonhomie that prevailed, but knew I had to eventually. I then decided that that was the operative word and that procrastination was the appropriate course of in-action.

The next few days passed in a whirl of introductions, visits to the laboratories, and other offices. While all this activity was going on, Merrill mentioned, in an off-hand manner, that he had thought of what he considered a fair salary figure and passed to me a newspaper he had been reading. I read in the margin a penciled amount of some considerable magnitude. I tried hard to be nonchalant: "Er, that's most generous," was all I could manage.

He grinned and said, "Well, if Roscoe makes his paint work we'll all be rich."

Back in my office I immersed myself in the pile of correspondence that had been waiting to be dealt with. The content, as well as the quantity, was impressive, ranging from enquiries from government agencies to well-known and prestigious commercial giants all anxious to receive more information and samples of this miraculous product.

The following week, as Merrill had promised, we were to go to Chicago for a meeting with the designer. I was really looking forward to meeting this man, as he was well known for his daring and unusual work and for his reputation for outspoken and sometimes abrasive commentaries on the contemporary design scene. I came down the stairs from my office to the entrance hall to find an impatient Merrill waiting. "Hurry Ed, there's a storm front coming in. We've got to get ahead of it, otherwise it's going to be a rough ride."

He drove, not recklessly, but fast and with a casual, flippant sort of way, one finger on the steering column, puffing the inevitable cigarette dangling from his lips, eyes alert, glancing everywhere.

After about fifteen minutes we swung off the highway and went up a dirt lane, through a gate, and stopped at a corrugated iron shed. We got out, collected our bags and some paraphernalia to do with aviation, navigation, and other matters aeronautical, and walked over to the buildings that housed the plane. As we approached, an elderly man, evidently the mechanic came out wiping his hands on an oily rag. "Hey Merrill how yer doin'?"

"okay."

"Everything ready? We're in a hurry. I don't like the look of that lot." He pointed in the direction of the western horizon, where foreboding black clouds were building.

"Yep, all set. She's in good shape." He turned to the shed door and pulled it open revealing a small monoplane on a tricycle undercarriage. Merrill approached, bent under the wing and opened a small door. He climbed up and disappeared.

"C'mon Ed, let's go." I quickly followed and gingerly mounted the wing. It was small and neat inside with dual controls and a mass of instruments clustered on a contoured dashboard. Merrill was already fiddling with knobs and switches. I sat there nervously wondering what to do when he handed me a clipboard. "Here," he growled, "read off the check list." I did as bid and commenced reading the long list of reminders.

This took a moment or two, when suddenly the engine started with a bang, gave a couple of pops, a cough or two, and roared into life. He played with the throttle and the motor settled into a contented purr. We taxied out of the building and rolled out onto the grass field. We stopped for a while at one end of a mown runway and he raised the throttle until the plane was straining against the brakes. He looked around and up to the sky and said, "Belted in? All set?"

"Yes Merrill," I answered, trying to sound calm.

He looked at me and grinned, "You'll be okay. Here we go." He released the brakes and we were off, careening down the green path. Out of the corner of my eye I watched the needle moving up as speed increased. We bumped and slid, faster and faster. A line of low trees got closer and closer. "Shouldn't we be up by now?" I thought. "Oh dear." The dark green wall came nearer.

"Holy Shit!" said Merrill, and with a final exertion pulled the control stick as far back as it would go. I heard a clatter as we brushed the tree tops then a whine and a clunk as the undercarriage locked up. We banked to the right and started to climb. I started to laugh with relief.

Once we were at cruising altitude Merrill began to speak into the mike at his throat. "Truax field, Truax field, this is Bonanza number, so and so," his call sign. Some radio jargon followed. He stopped and turned to me. "I had you going down there for a while," he said, "It's okay. You're in good hands with me, I've been flying since '42 in the Pacific." He went on to tell me bits of his naval aviation career. It was impressive. I was relieved and annoyed at the same time. I had been scared, but that was the way he was. I felt that somehow it had been a test and I had passed.

He talked again to the radio, calling Chicago for landing instructions, weather, and visibility. We were landing at a small aerodrome called Meigs field. It was right downtown, stuck out into the lake. It was for use by private aircraft only.

The sprawl of the city was beginning to appear ahead. It was now late afternoon and there was a ground mist which, with the sun glaring behind, created an illusion of theatricality to the downtown area, the skyscrapers looming out of the low white cotton wool, glinting, copper, bronze and obsidian.

We gently lost altitude and soon were turning into the final approach. The buildings that had appeared so distant and ethereal were now higher than we were and closer than seemed proper. Merrill appeared calm enough and after his admonition, I had decided to relax and enjoy. He was still talking and listening to the controllers even as we touched down. The lake sparkled and shone to my right. I felt a great surge of excitement and anticipation as we taxied slowly to the parking area.

I got out first and Merrill handed the bags to me. "okay Ed, now we're going to have some fun. Hey Betty. How the hell are you?" He was looking past me. I turned to see an enormous pink Cadillac convertible with the top down. Leaning against it, a pretty blonde woman.

"Hey Merrill you son-of-a-bitch, how are you? Who's your good looking friend?" Merrill made the introductions while I blushed and stammered.

"He's a Limey so be gentle with him honey. Where's Bob?"

"He had to go to St. Louis, but should meet us later."

"Betty, we're dry and hungry. Pick a place to eat. Anywhere."

"Anywhere?" she asked. "Sure. okay. The Buttery at the Ambassador East."

"Jeez Betty, you sure can pick 'em. okay. Take us to the hotel and we'll get washed up. We can have drinks there before we eat."

We pulled up at the front of the restaurant some time later. Merrill was quite tight by this time, having consumed an impressive amount of gin at the hotel, but was still in high spirits and was laughing and talking a mile a minute. The uniformed doorman saluted dramatically and flung open the large glass door.

"Good evening senator," he said. This was the nickname the world of service had bestowed on Merrill, who was a lavish tipper.

"Hey Matt, good to see you." A discreet sleight of hand followed, as largesse was delivered. We entered the foyer. There was more bowing and scraping as we crossed the room to the restaurant itself. The captain made a most undignified beeline for us and practically turned inside out in his efforts to make us welcome. "This way senator, this way. Your favourite table, of course. Nothing too good for you and your friends." The task of tipping was to fall to me later, but for now Merrill handled it, frequently and generously.

Sitting at the table was in itself a salutary experience with a flock of waiters hovering about, placing napkins on laps, lighting cigarettes with a flourish, proffering wine lists, which Merrill waved aside.

"Jesus Christ. None of that frog shit. Bring us double martinis." Dinner was elaborate and rich; the courses varied and interspersed with calls for more drinks and much banter. We all smoked between mouthfuls in the unhealthy manner of that day. Merrill was now getting increasingly incoherent as the liquor took hold. Betty and I were getting on wonderfully.

She was terrific company, funny, vivacious, and full of mischief. I was hoping husband might not turn up at all. At that moment there was a gurgling sound and Merrill in the most repulsive way, was sick down the front of his shirt. Instantly the waiters sprung into action. They mopped with napkins soaked in soda water, they wiped with dry cloths, they sprinkled some powder and mopped again, generally making an enormous fuss of this revolting incident.

I had sprung up, not knowing quite what to do. Betty had lit a cigarette and was calmly looking at her fingernails. Merrill pushed all the help out of the way, and snarled for a taxi.

"Shit, Ed, you and Betty shouldn't have your evening spoilt by me. Here," throwing me what looked like a wet green tennis ball.

"Take care of the bill and take Betty out on the town. Show Ed Rush Street, Betty." He staggered to his feet and, helped by two waiters, tottered out of the room.

"What did he give you?" asked Betty. I turned my attention to the paper ball. It was a tightly scrunched up wad of money, mostly fifties and twenties and amounting to almost a thousand dollars.

"Alright," said Betty, "Pay the bill and let's get out of here." The rest of the night passed in a whirl of bars, clubs, music, dancing, drinking, and behavior of a riotous fashion. I began to believe that the streets of America were paved with gold after all. I crawled back to the room at about four thirty to find a recovered Merrill shaving.

"Hey Ed get a bit of shut eye. We take off at six for Indianapolis." I fell into bed with a groan. The last thing I heard was Merrill chuckling to himself.

The rest of the trip was relatively uneventful. We did the Indianapolis thing. The designer meeting never did come off as he got hung up with something else, so the whole matter got postponed until another time.

We were now back in Wisconsin nearing the home field and were low, circling the area. It was amazing how hard it was to locate a small strip of grass, unless one was really familiar with the surroundings. Merrill of course was, and was already lowering the wheels while I was still gazing around trying to locate where we were.

The course of action we always followed when coming in to land was to buzz the house on one side of the river. When a porch light would come on, signifying our arrival had been noticed, someone would drive over to pick us up. This time there was, no light. Around we went, back to circling, then back to the house and so on until I was getting dizzy and slightly airsick. Finally the lamp flickered on and off. We made for the field. Merrill's wife Maggy was there to meet us. She explained cheerfully that she had been on the pot, they both laughed.

I really enjoyed that period with Merrill and that whole gang. They had lots of money and knew how to live and enjoy it. We worked hard and long hours, but it was exciting and rewarding. I learnt a lot about American business practices and a lot about the magic paint. Sadly it never really worked. It transpired that after a certain temperature was reached the material became unstable and destroyed itself.

Efforts were now made to save the company by substituting ingredients in the formula and we struggled on for some time managing to replace the original exciting idea with another product that was neither exciting or in the end worthwhile.

The next few months were spent in an atmosphere of mutual acrimony between marketing and research development and manufacturing.

⁕ ⁕ ⁕ ⁕

I had, during this time, acquired a small flat that looked over a lake in a pretty little spa town called Oconomowoc. It was green and quaint with friendly people who opened their doors and their hearts to me. I made many friends and there were parties galore. When I wasn't busy with work I played with the neighbours.

There were pool parties, country club dances, parties that were dress up, and parties that were casual to the extreme. We played tennis, sailed on the lake, had barbecues, drank excessively, and in general, grasped life with zest. We would make up groups and go zooming off to Milwaukee, which was the nearest large city, and there take a large table in the Pfister Hotel and behave in an unseemly and irresponsible way.

Jay, Charles Brady and the girls: the Milwaukee gang

It was at one of these gatherings that I met two people who were to become my best chums and who were to have some influence on my life and my future. Jay and Mona were attractive and elegant. He was a columnist with one of the city papers and she wrote reviews for a variety of technical publications. They were utterly charming, very sophisticated, and liked me. The feelings were mutual.

We were to spend a lot of time together. They introduced me to hordes of new people, including some very dishy girls I was to fall for romantically speaking, on a weekly basis. One girl whom I adored, a Mary Jane Marley, had a very chic flat where she gave smart cocktail parties. She had gorgeous auburn hair, thick, lustrous, and long. She was Junoesque in stature and captivated me utterly. She was unfortunately already spoken for, so my admiration was held at a respectful distance.

I kept up my end of the social whirl by giving regular parties, which became known as "Teddy's Thrashes," at my little flat in Oconomowoc. They were characterized by excessive drinking using vessels that ranged from some rather fine and elaborate glasses I had been given to jam jars and cracked and dusty tea mugs.

Mona Scriba and the boys in Milwaukee

My flat was shaped like a corridor. It was on the second floor of an old townhouse and sat on a long lot, grassed and sloping down to the edge of the lake that the town sat on, which was called Lac La Belle. The evenings always started with the best of manners and intentions, but invariably ended with a couple of fights, a broken marriage or two, and a lot of furtive sexual encounters on the shadowed lawn.

People came from as far as Chicago and there were often sleeping bodies under bushes next day that had to be attended to. The hangovers were legendary, caused probably by the homemade punches that Paul, the bartender from the hotel, made. They were mostly bourbon with pineapple juice with a splash of gin. It was called Ginsky. It was deadly, packing a punch like the kick from a mule. It probably didn't help that he mixed it in a none-too-clean waste paper basket he found in my kitchen.

I was dating intermittently, two girls at the time, Kathy who worked in my office and was pretty, blonde, and delicate, and a sexy cheerleader type, Myrna, who was bouncy, curvy, and utterly seductive. On the occasional time that they came to the same party, sparks would fly quite spectacularly.

I had by this time started looking for another job. The paint project was going nowhere. It was tragic really. It originally had such promise. The plans were that it could be used as a heat source domestically and commercially. A railway tank car had transported chocolate in liquid form across the country successfully and economically. It had been tested in high altitude rocketry that was then so much in the news.

In retrospect, Merrill was a sort of latter day Howard Hughes, a somewhat eccentric, high-flying, entrepreneur whom I was grateful to have had something to do with. However, we then entered a period of inconclusiveness.

Merrill was at daggers drawn with the manufacturing and research people, who he felt had led him down the garden. At a meeting in Chicago, which I attended, insults and accusations were hurled across the room. Just as I thought physical violence was about to occur, Roscoe and the R&D chaps got up in a huff and left the room leaving a stream of papers and the smell of acrimony behind.

Merrill said, "Fuck 'em. They'll be back," but they didn't return. "okay what now?" He turned to the company lawyer whose name was Neville and who I had never really liked. He was small and pallid with a weak damp handshake and eyes that were too close together.

"Cut your losses Merrill. Close the plant and shut them out."

"Gee, I don't want to do that." I felt very sorry for him. At that moment he looked so defeated and bewildered. He'd had such faith in the product and had spent so much money. "Well, let's go and have a drink and dinner and sleep on it."

As we flew back to head office next morning it was a quiet and thoughtful man who sat next to me. No affable comments bordering on the slanderous about other aircraft sharing air space with us, especially those commercial ones, which he thought took up too much space even if we were nowhere near them in altitude. We circled the house as usual. This time Maggy came out at once and waved.

✻ ✻ ✻ ✻

One morning Merrill called me in his office and told me to prepare for a flight to Angola, Indiana, where the factory was located, He said, "I've decided to cut my losses and close the goddamn place down. There's some stuff, samples and papers and such. I want you to pack everything up and bring it back here. There's a pickup truck you can use." I must say I didn't relish this, but thought it better to concur. He was obviously in no mood to cross that day.

We drove out to the field and took off for Indiana, It was a quick flight and soon we were circling the area where we thought the little field was, where we were to land. Again, it was remarkable how difficult it is to find a small rural landing ground in the middle of nowhere. Finally we did locate the place. It was getting dark, so I was relieved when we touched down and taxied to a small Quonset hut.

Merrill switched off and gave me his final orders. I was to locate the caretaker who had the keys and have him gain entrance for me. He gave me a list of what he wanted.

It was a considerable quantity of sample hush-hush material, formulas, also secret, and files and files of valuable data.

"Good luck Ed. See you in a couple of days. Don't fuck around too long down here. We need the stuff in Jefferson quickly." It was with dismay that I watched the little aeroplane take off and disappear into a darkening sky.

I turned to the hut. There was a light in the window. I walked in to find a group of men sitting around a pot-bellied stove. They looked around, "Can I get a cab into town?"

"Oh hi," said one. "You just came in the Bonanza?"

"Yes." I explained that I needed to get to the plant and told them where it was.

"Oh sure the Thermaflex place. We can get you there. Cabs don't exist around here after dark. Like a drink?" He produced a bottle of Jim Beam. I noticed then that they were all drinking out of paper cups.

"Sure" I said. It was just what I needed. We had a couple of quick ones and then left for town. It had to be about ten by the time we arrived. I planned to collect the stuff and load it up and be on my way that night, perhaps getting as far as the south side of Chicago by midnight. I was in for the nightmare of my life.

We looked at the closed-up and silent factory building. It was a small single storey structure. We walked around to the front door. I looked for sounds or sight of a night watchman. There was none. The place was abandoned and locked up. How to get in? Merrill had neglected to give me keys.

One of my newfound chums had a flashlight and we examined the door locks. "Well, we can easily break in," said one.

"Break in?" I said nervously.

"Looks like the only way Ed." We were on first name basis.

"W-e-e-l-l," I hesitated. There was a creaking noise and the sound of splintering wood. A dog barked in the distance. I realized I needed to pee. While we hesitated, one of the others had the door broken and open, hanging on its hinges. Joe, for that was the leader's name, flashed the torch around. We were in a hall that led to an office and then to the assembly line area beyond. I found the filing cabinets and started to go through the files, and realizing this would take all night decided to take everything. We got boxes and started to load up.

"Well, we've gotta go. The wives will be wondering where we are." I looked at my watch. It was almost midnight.

"Thanks fellers. I don't know what I'd have done without your help."

"You're welcome. Sure you'll be alright?"

Though I was far from feeling confident that I would be all right, I knew that I couldn't prevail on their kindness any more. We had already broken several laws as it was. They left and I was alone. I found the pick-up truck and thanked God it had gas in the tank. But no filler cap. I stuffed a rag into the hole and looked it over. It was an old beat-up Ford that had seen better days.

Again I was in luck. There was a key in the ignition. I got in, stamped on the gas a couple of times and turned it. The whole rig shuddered and shook as the engine exploded into life. I let it run for a bit and switched off. I now set off to find the sample units. Not an easy job in the semi-darkness and I had to work fast before it got light and someone came investigating. Luckily it wasn't long before I located them: about ten units measuring four by eight feet. They were light in weight fortunately.

I quickly got them in the truck, lashed them down alongside all the boxes of files, and covered the whole lot with a tarpaulin. I looked around to see if there was anything else that might be of use or that Merrill might like to have, but decided not to pursue this line as the torch was starting to dim and flicker. I pulled the door together as best I could and got into the truck. As I pulled out onto the highway and headed north, I looked at my watch. It was two a.m.

After an hour's driving I had reached a place with an ominous reputation, Gary, Indiana. This was where the steel and rolling mills were. A tough mean area of grey smoking chimneys, of sooty caliginous intensity, not a place to be driving through at that time and in my circumstances of some fragility and ineptness.

At that moment there was a dull pop and the truck slewed to one side of the road and sank gently to one side, I had a flat rear tire. 'Oh God, was there a spare? Could I fix it?'

I stopped the engine and dismounted. It was still dark and raining lightly. Streetlights lit the darkness and I could see that I was in a totally industrial neighbourhood. There wouldn't be anyone around to help me. My heart sank. I turned back to the tire. Flat as a pancake. And there was no spare.

At that moment of despair, around a nearby corner, a large white car came screeching. It came to a precipitate stop alongside the truck and an enormous black man got out.

"Hey, how er yeh doin'?"

"Er, not too good I'm afraid. A flat and no spare."

The black face split with a smile of incandescent whiteness. "Jump in my car. There's a gas station up the road. They'll fix it for yeh."

I mumbled my thanks and got in the back. The car's interior was red leather and smelt of it and of a heavy but pleasant musky perfume. The other occupants, I hadn't noticed before, were two young women with pretty black faces. They smiled and said "Hi."

"Er hi. Er hello." I replied.

"What in the hell are you, a white guy, and a Limey by the sound of you, doin' in this goddam hellhole?"

I explained my predicament.

He laughed and said, "You're lucky we came along. This ain't no neighbourhood for white folks to break down. Here's the garage." We pulled up. He got out with me and walked to the office.

"Hey Joe." The men in the place jumped up. The feeling of obsequious respect was palpable. He was obviously someone in this world of darkness and danger.

"Fix my friend's flat and make it snappy."

"Sure Joe, no problem. Any friend of Joe's is okay by us," etc., etc.

Joe turned to me and said "You white folk in England during the war were kind and friendly to me when I was a G.I. Consider this a 'thank you.' " He turned and went out into the gloom. The work was done in double-quick time and I was soon on my way through downtown, which in those days was the only way through the city.

Everything went all right until I reached the north end of town, the part they call the Gold Coast. Here I had another flat and the manual gearshift refused to enter fourth gear. Luckily I was within walking distance of a repair garage and it was light. I paid in advance for a new tire. The gears would have to remain fourthless. I found a place to have breakfast while the work was done.

I reached home office during the middle of the day

to receive a grumpy "What took you so long?" I decided in the wisdom of silence.

❋ ❋ ❋ ❋

This interlude seemed to reflect the rags to riches formula presented those Saturdays so long ago at the cinema by the Zanucks and Goldwyns and Selznicks, There was a documentary made recently about the history of these eastern European refugees escaping the pogroms of Russia and other persecutions and cruelties inflicted on them by their oppressive masters. These penniless but talented immigrants found their way to the western Americas and began the movie business as we know it today, creating the picture of the American way of life, the dream, the life of plenty, the pictures of Andy Hardy and the girl next door, the hopes and fears of Walter Mitty, the adventures of Tyrone Power and Errol Flynn, The Spanish Main, and the romanced cowboy and Indian had their inspiration far away in a snowy frigid hut on the steppes of the country of their birth.

❋ ❋ ❋ ❋

My attempts for new employment were not meeting with success until one evening when I walked into the little local hotel's bar for a drink before dinner. It was a small, cozy, dimly lit room, comfortably furnished and smelling of wax and cigar smoke. The bartender was an amusing alcoholic Boston Irishman who had taken a fancy to me and would address me as "My lord," and would introduce me to newcomers as an aristocratic Englishman living as a sort of remittance man in the colonies.

His form of welcome to me was always "Good evening m' lord. Shall we light the lamps tonight?" which was code for a dry martini made with lamplighter gin. He had a hilarious way of, when pouring cocktails for customers, using a sleight of hand, to give himself a slug of whatever the liquor was, all done with great finesse and circumspection. He and his wife and I spent many hours of gentle inebriation together. They were both highly intelligent and well informed. Many were the problems, political and domestic, that we solved.

It was through him that I met, in the bar, my future employer. He was a sales manager for a large paint and varnish company in Michigan that supplied the car industry, the domestic appliance industry, and the furniture manufacturing business. He almost fell off the stool when we were introduced.

"You're English," he said, eyes wide open. I

admitted that fact. "This is amazing," he said. "We've been looking for someone to replace our colour stylist Dan Greevy who just died. He was a Brit, and we wanted to continue that tradition. Do you know anything about paint and or colour in the fashion sense?"

I told him about my art background, exaggerating slightly my acute sense of colour and appreciation for good taste in home furnishings. He seemed impressed. "Hell, we can teach you the chemical side of paint coatings and formulations. I think you might be just the guy."

I loved this aspect of the American character. Ready to take people at face value, quick to hold out an open hand, so unlike the British reserve and suspicion. "I will call my principals in the morning and arrange an interview. How about a nightcap? Set 'em up Paul." With a wink at me, Paul filled, stirred, and poured the drinks, giving himself an extra large share which he downed before our glasses touched the bar top. What a guy.

A week had passed without a word and when I had to go to New York on business for Merrill, I went in a rather gloomy frame of mind. However, while showering before dinner, the telephone rang, and answering, I heard with pleasure, George Ehrett's voice, for that was the name of the paint man. "Swell, we've tracked you down. Can you come to Grand Rapids to meet the folks here next week?" I said that I could the next day, on my return flight to Milwaukee. "That's even better. Everyone is looking forward to meeting you."

I was elated. I had to share this promising news with somebody. Dare I call Laura? I had not heard from her since that awful afternoon at the Plaza. Dare I? *He* might answer. What would I say? I swallowed, trying to still the waves of doubt that filled me. I'll hang up if he does. Damn. Do it.

I dialed, the phone rang twice, and her lovely warm husky voice came on. "Laura, it's me, Teddy."

"My God I've been thinking of you. This is fantastic. Where are you?"

"I'm here in town."

"Here in Manhattan?"

"Yes."

"God, I've got to see you."

I shivered with pleasure.

"Where are you staying?"

"The Prince George on 34th St.

"Yes, right. I'll be there in thirty minutes. There's a nice bar in the basement. Meet me there."

I floated down to the lobby and found the little bar. It was perfect. Low lights, almost empty. I ordered a martini and lit a cigarette. I was trembling with anticipation. Right on time, she arrived, beautiful, chic, laughing, her perfume combined with the scent of the cold open air at night. We hugged and kissed, taking no notice of the waiter who was hovering nearby. We finally released each other and sat holding hands, spellbound and speechless. She said, "God, I need a drink. Is that a martini? I'll have the same. Waiter. With a twist."

She turned to me, "Teddy, I know you won't believe this, but I was going to mail this tomorrow." She passed me a crumpled envelope stamped and sealed. "I know this is all wrong, but I've missed you so much, and was asking you to meet me somewhere."

Damn, this was all too marvelous for words. "Can you stay with me tonight?" I asked.

"No, but I can tomorrow."

Damn and double damn. I told her of the interview tomorrow in Grand Rapids.

"But surely you can put that off?" Her lovely eyes pleaded.

I looked at her wonderful face and thought of all the times I had dreamt of such a moment. I examined every detail thinking that if I didn't make the right decision I might never see her again. This was desperately hard, but I knew that the right thing to do is always the hard thing to do, so said 'no,' that I had to keep the appointment, and that I was certain that I would be back.

She sighed and sat back. "okay, I guess I'd better get back, Dick and Bruce will be wondering where I am."

I had a deflating feeling of déjà vu. Walking down the steps to a waiting cab, I was in the depths of depression. We both agreed that we would try to meet again soon, but my heart was heavy. The cab disappeared in the rain and gloom and I returned to my room to ponder my decision. Bogart and Bergman. Oh the tears of the silver screen, the vicissitudes of romance.

❋ ❋ ❋ ❋

The next day I flew to Michigan to meet the president and directors of the company. All the interviews seemed to go well and at noon we all trooped off to their club. It was called The Peninsula and was in the British tradition, leather armchairs, wood paneling and a hushed atmosphere. We were directed, with much ceremony, to a large round table and sat down.

I looked around a room of gargantuan proportions, heavily curtained, large high windows, mirrors everywhere that attenuated the dimensions of the room, a buzz of conversation coming from the other tables already fully occupied, the whole scene redolent with the scent of burning tobacco and the sound of clinking glasses.

After a delicious meal of some length, preceded by several double Manhattans, we returned to the offices, where I was introduced to more important executives and finally to the chairman, who was a crusty old gent with a lined leathery face, suspicious eyes, and a scowling mouth.

The first thing he said was that he didn't like Limeys and then grilled me for about half an hour. I barely held my own. What, with the food and drink I had just had, I was more in the mood for a nap than a cross-examination. I was somehow able to satisfy him, for, after a few more questions, he seemed to tire of the whole business and indicated that the interview was at an end. I left the room feeling shaken.

"Don't worry Ed. He's a tough old bird. The fact that he didn't throw you out is a positive sign. Now, we've reserved a room at the Cambridge Hotel downtown. Go and have a rest or look around the city. We'll pick you up at six tonight. You meet the wives at the country club. They have to give you the once over too." I collapsed on the bed in the quite sumptuous room they had got for me, and fell into a heavy sleep of relief and exhaustion.

The evening that followed was relaxed and enjoyable. The wives seemed to approve of me, especially as I liked to dance and this was a recreation not shared by middle-aged, middle-western, businessmen of substance. They, in fact, appeared to relish that they could be spouseless for a moment or two and engage in banter of a crude sexual nature, so I was made much of by the ladies who gave the impression of being starved of attention of any sort. As I also enjoyed flirtation, this made the evening even more fun.

The first thing next day, prior to take-off for home,

I had a brief but positive conversation with George, who indicated that I had the job, but that he would confirm by mail in a few days. We left each other with warm wishes. I climbed aboard the plane and flew back to Wisconsin.

* * * *

These last few weeks had been interesting, sometimes a little too hectic, and mostly spent in the company of successful and comfortably off men and women. There was another side to the American picture where the dream had not, however, been achieved and where the attitudes of those that had everything did not include any compassion for those that had nothing, and where self-aggrandizement was paramount and any sympathy for the poor white or black, was non-existent.

I noticed as well the little interest in matters of international importance. This part of the world had been isolationist in the thirties and had many people of German and Nordic extraction living there now. They were almost to a man, Republican, and rabidly anti-Roosevelt, who they considered wicked and somehow involved in the entanglements with Japan leading to the disaster at Pearl Harbour. I tried to explain the British veneration for this President and how, without the help of America, our prospects would have been dim indeed. This only made them more vexed, so I gave up and chose my companions with care.

Many of the other opinions held by these pillars of the community were patronizing, uninformed and troubling. Their knowledge of matters outside their immediate ken was abysmally ignorant and I had to struggle to hold my tongue to these otherwise kind and hospitable folk.

Another aspect of the contemporary scene was that the surroundings themselves, that part of the States, are not seen at their best in wintertime. For it was now November, gloomy and grey. Although the big cities are impressive and architecturally exciting, the little towns are generally featureless, grimy, and possess little of interest. Advertising hoardings abound. Filling stations, hopeless tawdry little shops, and ugly wooden homes, invariably painted white, bristling with TV aerials, proliferate. In the downtown section, movie theatres, garish with neon, posters adorning the stained walls with peeling promises of attractions to come, the smell of popcorn, and Wrigley's chewing gum fill the air. Cheek by jowl, bowling alleys lurked, and bars advertising beers with ungainly names like Blatz, Schlitz, and Budweiser, that are described in a kind of shorthand for the English language as draft and lite, send a message that is both forlorn and unwelcoming. The doors spasmodically open to allow a customer who has wined and dined too well to be ejected by the management.

At one time I was shown an area of Chicago referred to as 'Skid Row.' It fascinated and repelled me. A long street with wide pavements lined by bars and loan shops, pawn shops, and cheap doss-house-type hotels, neon-lit again, but with many of the tubes empty of gas, so flickering, as if transmitting a message of despair. Mostly men. I don't remember seeing any women. Mostly men, and mostly incapacitated by drink. They leaned, sat, lay, and slouched, their heads in paper bags that contained the libation of choice, mostly, I learnt, cheap sweet sherry.

Loud sounds of argument, cursing and smashing glass filled the evening air as we drove slowly by, followed by looks of resentment and hostility. A police cruiser pulled out and passed us, siren wailing. These sad and melancholy scenes had certainly been a large part of my cinema memories. Paul Muni and Edward G. Robinson, George Raft and others parading around as Scarface. The Mean Streets, the danger, the desolation, the despair of drink.

* * * *

Back home I had to tell my family of my plans, and of course explain to Merrill why I was leaving. He was very understanding but downcast. I felt guilty and was genuinely sorry at having to abandon him, but he knew that the company was not going anywhere and did in fact, I heard later, start up another business. Madeleine and Bob were equally sad at my forthcoming departure, though I was not going to be too far away, just across Lake Michigan, and would visit on a regular and frequent basis.

The next few days were spent making my goodbyes. I had liked living in Wisconsin. The little town I lived in was the exception to the rule that I described earlier, and was both attractive and surrounded by pretty rolling country. The people were hospitable and friendly, the nearby city Milwaukee, exciting and lively. I looked forward however, to new scenery and new faces.

I had bought a second-hand English sports car, a Morgan, brilliant and powerful, in Italian racing vermilion. Most of the body encased a raucous engine, a compact two seat driving compartment and a tiny cramped luggage space.

Fortunately the company was paying for moving my furniture, so all I had to squeeze in were personal items of clothing and articles of necessity, which included a small flask of scotch and Siegfried Sassoon's "Memoirs of a Fox

Hunting Man."

I was to travel by cross-lake car ferry, which sailed out of Milwaukee for the port of Ludington, an overnight journey. Later that day I was nervously steering the car up a ramp and entering a cavernous hold to join a few other automobiles that were already lashed down. The lake could be quite rough in winter and was to prove so later when we sailed that evening.

I stood on the upper deck watching the activity that reminded me of my navy days. I was lost in nostalgic thoughts when a loud siren's hoot broke the spell. The ship was starting to move away from the jetty, first astern, then after stopping, shaking, and shuddering, then moving ahead, all the static objects, buildings, cranes, and other shore paraphernalia gliding past. As we hit the open lake the wind came up and the boat began to pitch and roll. I found a lounge and lay down. How absurd. I felt seasick. I made a beeline for the toilets to find them already full of other suffering passengers. After an interminable and disturbing night, dawn found us entering a small harbour. With great relief we all disembarked.

The first impressions were encouraging. I drove through rolling forested country that looked both prosperous and well husbanded. There were few built up areas, a few farmhouses with black and white cattle just like Wisconsin. It was a relatively short drive to Grand Rapids. Early afternoon saw me checking into a motel on the edge of town. After a good night's sleep, I reported to head office.

I was taken everywhere and shown everything. I met sales people, production heads, people who counted profits and losses and paid wages and salaries, chemists and back room boys, vague and otherworldly. I toured the plants where paint boiled and fumed in vats of vast proportions, viscous and colourful, stirred by propellers and attended by goggled, masked operators gazing intently at dials and indicators. The smell of solvents and other acrid materials smarted the eyes and irritated the throat.

Finally I was introduced to the staff of the so-called studio, which was to be where I was to be taught my new undertaking. They were called "colour stylists" and worked at the task of creating new finishes for the automobile, furniture, and appliance industries. They, in effect, were the experts that were consulted by the fashion gurus when it came to the "in" colours of the day. Close liaison was kept with other design people, the interior magazines, especially House & Garden, who annually introduced their choices for the colours of the day.

After my training period, I was to be the head stylist. The title I was given was "Colour Consultant," a label that caused an ancient relative of mine to think I was doing good work among the natives in some colony. No amount of explanation would disabuse her of this fancy.

There was another aspect to the work done, and

that was to the continuing developmental experiments to produce a clear coating that would withstand all the vicissitudes of everyday life, whether the coated article was a car, a refrigerator or a piece of wooden furniture.

I was also shown my new office that was large and magnificent, carpeted and filled with expensive looking period antiques. I found afterwards that they were in fact fakes, or as they preferred to call them, reproductions. This, apparently, was the main part of my job, to have a substantial knowledge relating to furnishings of a variety of periods, create colours with stains and glazes, formulate the recipes, so that they could be expanded into thousands of gallons and pounds, take them into furniture factories and teach the conveyor line operatives how to reproduce our examples en masse.

Some of the conveyors ran at the amazing speed of 20 odd feet a minute. All the various steps, which sometimes amounted to 12, had to be applied by spray gun and by hand. Most of these factories were located in the south, North Carolina, and Virginia, so a lot of my time was to be spent traveling. I also had to spend time in the centres of design such as New York, Chicago, and San Francisco. I knew that I was going to like this job.

Eventually the training period was completed. I had learnt about the basics of colour chemistry and paint technology, a considerable amount of information relating to the history of furniture, the kind of woods used, both veneered and solid, a fair bit about construction and manufacturing of wood furnishings, some knowledge of finishing equipment, and the complexities of design and application. It was another matter to put all this to some useful purpose.

* * * *

It was now high summer and I discovered how hot and humid it could become in this part of the world. Working in the studio or in my office was comfortable, with air conditioning, but the factories, where I spent so much time, were insufferably hot, not like the Sudan, which had been hot but dry, this was like being in a hothouse, sultry and clammy. The day's ending, with its comparative coolness, was welcome. We would all repair to some local hostelry and consume vast amounts of Michelob draught beer.

It had been decided that, as so many of the furniture plants had gone south, largely to escape the demands of unions looking for a better deal for their members, I should move there too and take over a new studio facility at our plant in High Point in the Carolinas. The transfer would take place in about six months when the construction would be completed. Meanwhile, there was plenty to do to occupy me here and I continued to grow and become more confident in my job and generally as a foreigner in a new country.

The attitudes toward me were mostly positive and friendly. I was invited to lots of parties, many of them beside pools and involving much drinking of Bloody Marys and eating of barbecued hot dogs and hamburgers which were deliciously juicy and messy, with sauces, chopped onions, pickles, and slices of tomato. I had met several attractive young women, but not one who could erase the memory of Laura, who I missed dreadfully. I noticed as well that I was frequently the target of unhappy married women. My European background, good manners, and willingness to listen were unfortunately a combination much esteemed by these sad, but still vibrant and appealing ladies, whose husbands had abandoned them for the golf course.

It was at one of these gatherings that the hostess said "Oh Teddy you'll want to meet Jamie. He's a countryman of yours. He's out walking in the woods. Help yourself to a drink." There was lots of hard stuff on the bar but no beer and I really felt like one.

I went to the fridge and opened it. There was one can of lager. I opened it and was drinking it gratefully when a stocky red-faced man entered the kitchen. He ignored me and went straight to the refrigerator. He peered inside and I heard, "Bugger, where's my beer?" He looked at the can and me and said, "I was looking forward to that." The accent was unmistakable upper-class English.

I said, "I hear you're a fellow countryman."

"Oh, what makes you think that?"

"Well, I'm English."

"I'm Scottish," was his terse reply, He turned on his heel and disappeared.

Next day I was in my office preparing some wood panels we used for presentation to customers when the telephone rang. It was the Scotsman, "I say, I'm sorry I was rude yesterday. Margaret, my wife, said that I was insufferable. Sorry. Would you like to come to dinner tonight?"

Thus began a friendship with a remarkable man, born into the Scottish aristocracy and bearing a lineage that went back to Joan of Norway and latterly Robert the Bruce: James Bruce Sandilands, Master of Torphichen, and who was now teaching history in a school of some repute in Grand Rapids. He was extraordinarily well-educated, the classic combination of Eton and Balliol, one of the better Oxford colleges, had a life of academic brilliance, with some years in minor politics and journalism. He had been everywhere and knew everyone.

We took to each other, me to listen and learn, he to talk and guide. He had an infectious sense of humour and when we weren't arguing and debating, we were laughing, sometimes until the tears came. I loved this man and we were to spend many happy days together. He liked to drink and to party and although in a position of some dignity, was ever open and completely without snobbishness or false airs. Everyone adored him. His only drawback was a dislike of baths and a total disinterest in hygiene, but he was a genius and being near him was worth the occasional whiff of B.O.

I had also met some people who were sports car mad and members of the Sports Car Club of America. They prevailed on me to join and to take part in small rallies and speed events they organized in the Grand Rapids area. My Morgan car was quite rare and attracted a good deal of interest and attention at all the functions in which I took part, one of which, a race on a frozen lake in the town, was especially notable. Volunteers had cleared a rudimentary track around it and round and round we went at dizzying speeds skidding and spinning in all directions. The beauty was that, other than the odd collision with another car, the banks were piled-up snow, and stopped one gently and satisfactorily. We also did hill climbs and generally had a blast.

* * * *

One of the couples I met I was specially fond of and they of me. She was sweet and looked like Doris Day. She became very well known in the Detroit area as a TV hostess and fashion guru. It was when we were together, one evening, having dinner at a downtown restaurant that I was to meet Susan Godstone.

I had just turned around to find a waiter when Elizabeth Taylor walked in. At least that's who she looked like. I knew the man who was with her, so quickly contrived an introduction and invited them to join us. We got on immediately, that marvelous feeling when chemistries work, the outside world disappears and one is lost to another, especially if they look as good as this. She had a great sense of the ridiculous and was soon laughing with the rest of us. Oh, this could be the one. Her friend was just that, a friend, so there was no resentment at my attentions. The evening broke up late and we promised to meet again.

I waited what I considered a suitable time before calling, not wanting to appear too callow, but when I reached her, found her friendly and eager to see me. She, in fact, asked me if I would like to spend the weekend at her family's lakeshore cabin. I relished the thought of being with this lovely girl for two days and nights, but, a cabin, her family? I was doubtful.

I imagined some dank log house with bugs and outside plumbing and two elderly parents keeping a sharp and dubious eye on their precious daughter and me. Hmm. Susan was adamant. She said "you'll love it, we can swim and sail and sunbathe," (none of these recreations particularly appealed to me) but I agreed to go. I had nothing else planned and was, to boot, a bit skint. I had been spending too much lately, so this would be a cheap couple of days. Well, was I going to get a surprise.

That Friday evening we drove to Northport where the cabin was. The trip took about three hours so that it was dark when we arrived. The town was on a small peninsula jutting out into Lake Michigan at the most northern point of the state. We drove down a tree-lined street, the occasional house standing well back from the road, lights burning in a cheerful welcoming way. Although it was dark, I could see that these were buildings of some substance. We came to a gate in a high brick wall and stopped. A uniformed guard came to the car and peered inside with a torch. "It's okay Bill. It's me, Susan."

"Oh, okay miss. Good evening. I'll open the gate." We passed through and entered an estate heavily wooded on one side and open to a sparkling lake on the other. An enormous house appeared as we crunched up a gravel drive.

"Here we are," she said and turned off the motor.

Here we were indeed, I thought, as I gazed with awe at this magnificent pile. This was a palace not a cabin. I learnt that this was their summerhouse and that the cabin for two was down by the beach. Spirits rose proportionately. Out from the now open front door flooding light to the outside, came an elderly servant, a sort of wrinkled retainer. His appearance belied his strength, for with no trouble at all, he swung our bags up and was away with them into the house, almost colliding with two people coming out. These were mama and papa, another surprise for the evening. "Susan darling, and your friend. Lovely. Come in. martinis are ready. Dinner in an hour." We were whisked into the house divested of outer coats and shown into a large and beautiful room.

It was all astonishing, the luxuriousness of the surroundings and the youthful attractiveness of the parents. They both looked like siblings of Susan. They were in fact not much older than me, early to mid-thirties. I realized that Susan had to be in her late teens, no older. This was a bit tricky. She was, however, very mature, and she was so pretty. Well let's enjoy the moment.

I found out afterwards that the family were inordinately wealthy, owned a large printing company and were in fact what Americans refer to as "old money." They were charming, cultured, and very with it. They were both tanned and fair and beautiful. I was entirely captivated. The sitting room reflected their taste. It was casually furnished in the way of a seaside retreat, white linen-covered arm chairs and divans, well-worn rugs on a simple pine floor, books everywhere, large curtained windows, now open to the lake breeze from outside. I sipped appreciatively on the perfect martini and thought, "Now I know there is gold in the streets."

After a scrumptious dinner of lobster and sweet corn washed down by some impeccable Sauterne, we were shown our quarters. These were in a small two-storey pine cabin that was sparely furnished, but comfortable and bright. It had separate bedrooms, a small sitting room, kitchen, and bathroom. It was perfect in every way. We spent a magical night together and next day rumpled the sheets in the unused room. I was, I thought, perhaps in love.

We spent the rest of the weekend exactly as she had said we would. The sun shone and the lake was calm. We swam and sailed, played tennis, drank wine, and made love. Sunday night came too soon and we had to return to town.

Back in the studio next day everyone was talking, as people do, about what they had done at the weekend. When it came to my turn and the name of the family I had been with came up, there was an astonished gasp. "Jesus Christ, Ed you've hit the jackpot." Everyone knew the Godstones. I was congratulated and given advice and from then on I was known as Ed The Vault.

Sadly, the state of affairs did not last. We really had little in common other than that that was physical. She was interested in the field of computers, then coming into the public eye, and spent much of her time studying and working. We spent less time together and when I realized that I found the mother more attractive than the daughter, decided that it was time to end the affair.

⁂ ⁂ ⁂ ⁂

I was getting closer to the time of departure for the south. It was near to autumn, and as I was driving and wanted to do the trip while the weather was good, I began winding up business and domestic details. Accommodation had been found for me in the city of Greensboro, which I had visited on earlier trips to North Carolina and which I thought seemed more attractive than High Point, where the plant and studio were located.

⁂ ⁂ ⁂ ⁂

Early one morning, after a long night of bibulous farewells, I set out in my tiny car loaded to the gunwales with all that I could squeeze in. It was a lovely clear day with a touch of frost. I felt elated and optimistic as we bowled down the highway. I was soon past Detroit and well into Ohio heading for the Pennsylvania turnpike. I went over, in my mind, the route I had planned to follow over the mountains to the highway that ran down the Shenandoah Valley, the road winding between high green hills until we reached Roanoke and then over more hills until we entered Virginia, then on, south, to North Carolina. The whole journey took over fifteen hours.

These were the days before four-lane highways, so driving times were considerably more than they are today, the mountain roads steep and winding, with spectacular views in all directions. I arrived in Greensboro early in the evening and found a motel for the night, I would check in the next day and find where my new place was.

The reception I got at the plant was mixed. The manager was a grumpy, older man, not particularly pleased to see me. There was a built-in resentment to the northern management group that was partly based on some personal enmity and partly on the still-existing prejudice stemming, I was amazed to discover, from the war between the States that had been fought some one hundred years before. I was told, after I'd been there a few weeks that I might be a God damned limey, but at least I wasn't a God damned Yankee. The rest of the staff was, on the whole, coolly friendly. I knew that I was going to have to prove myself and that was to be my first priority.

❋ ❋ ❋ ❋

The next few weeks were spent in finding my way around the area, settling in to my new flat, getting some additional furniture, and checking out the town and country surrounding the city. The coming days and weeks brought many surprises. I was to learn a lot about the south, its people, and their attitudes. On the whole, as time went by, they were hospitable and amiable to me.

England had been on their side during the Civil War, which helped. There was still a strong snobbish streak that ran through society. Old established families admired my country and its class distinctions. They recognized my accent as gentlemanly, so opened their doors to me and I made many friends. They treated their black servants kindly and they, in return, reacted in a respectful but non-servile manner. They seemed to like each other.

This was not the case as one went further down the pecking order. The resentful contemptuous way the blacks were dealt with among the poorer white classes was shocking in its intensity and its prevalence. One white foreman I was taking out to lunch from one of the plants said to me as we drove in his car, "D'you want to have a look at my nigger killer?" snapped open the glove compartment and brandished a gigantic shiny, nickel-plated revolver. I looked at him with horror. He laughed in the cruelest way. The meal was not a success, and I had to hold my tongue to stop myself losing the account, which was worth hundreds of thousands of dollars.

Other impressions were of the way feudalism still thrived in these valleys, the large palatial house on the hill, often with a Roll Royce in the drive, the factory, down deep in the shadowed vale, smoke belching out of tall grimy chimneys, a small village of ramshackle bungalows bristling with TV masts, and with refrigerators on the front porch, often side-by-side with a dilapidated sofa, a mongrel dog tied up, a rusting tireless car in the scratchy drive. On the main street, a company store and bank that the employees were forced to use, a bar or two, a church, a school. This was where the white folk lived, played, and worshipped. The black workers were around the corner out of sight behind the hill.

The food and drinking habits were other matters that required some adjustment on my part. Most of the food one was served in the better restaurants and cafés, which were few, was the common or garden sort seen everywhere in the US, heavy on the mashed potatoes and gravy, meat loaf, apple pie, chops, that sort of thing. Here one added the fried chicken, meat, potatoes, fish, and pretty well anything that had once moved or grew. Green salads were rare and the vegetables were unusual and slightly sinister, collard greens, the leaves of a spinach that must have grown in the back yards of poor folk, stunted objects that looked like corn that had been plucked too early and was hard and tasted like rancid flour.

Often, for some reason known only to them, these were served with something resembling tripe, called fat back or sow's belly. On the other hand there were delicious chicken stews and a dessert that was quite divine, peach cobbler. Drinking was heavily controlled. No spirits or wines could be served in a café or bar. One had to buy the booze at a government control centre and take it to the place of consumption in the brown bag in which it was sold, hide it under the table, and only pick it up when ice and water were served and the drink mixed, then the bottle was deposited back in the bag and replaced out of sight. It was a strange and anachronistic arrangement enforced by the Calvinistic attitudes of the southern clergy and their unlikely allies, the rumrunners.

On the positive side I had made a lot of new friends, many of them transplanted northerners, and was enjoying the work immensely. I had to travel to New York a lot to visit the large stores where I would meet with the designers and sales people to discuss fashion trends that changed frequently. At first I had to really wing it, my knowledge of fashion was, to say the least, spotty, but somehow or other I managed to keep up.

❋ ❋ ❋ ❋

One wonderful day I was told to go to San Francisco, a city I had long wanted to see. I was to go to Los Angeles too, as there were particular shops I had to visit in Beverley Hills.

I left early in the morning. It was January, so it was chilly, but not like Chicago where I had to change planes. Here it was bitterly cold with a snowstorm howling. The powers that be must have known something we didn't, for the flight was not cancelled as I thought it would be. In fact I had to run to get to the counter and check in. After going over my ticket and looking at the computer screen, the agent looked up and said "It's your lucky day, you are being bumped to first. Oversold in coach." She stamped a couple of papers, attached them to the boarding pass and said, "Have a nice trip."

As I entered the plane, I was greeted extravagantly and ushered forward to the cabin. It was opulent in an understated way, a grey leathery atmosphere, large armchair-like seats with space galore in front, behind, and on either side. There were not many passengers, so that it seemed we had two hostesses to each passenger. The two that attended me adjusted the seat back and belt, proffered magazines and smiles, brilliant in perfect, tanned, mascaraed, lip-sticked faces, and encouraged the consumption of Bollinger with orange juice if desired. I declined the latter and sipped on the former. A lighter flicked in front of my face and lit my Lucky Strike. The plane bumped along to its take-off position. I leaned back in heaven.

Take-off was a little dicey as the snow blowing made it difficult to see, but the wheels left the ground in a satisfactory manner and soon we were climbing through clouds that thinned and scattered as we rose. Suddenly, with an incandescent flash the cabin was filled with sunshine that made one blink. The lights were turned off and seat bells began to ring. No bells for us up front. We were pounced upon by these glamorous handmaidens and made much of.

The champagne and quite excessive lunch took its toll. I faded into a deep untroubled sleep. When I woke up we were in completely clear conditions and I could see the ground in all its colourful details. We were told we were over the Grand Canyon, which, from this altitude, looked like a terra cotta ditch.

As it got darker and we got closer to the destination, we were served more drink and more food. I washed face and hands and prepared myself for the arrival. Landing was smooth and deplaning fast and painless. I liked this first class stuff. I'd even got a phone number from the blonde hostess.

I was being met by one of the company's salesmen who looked after this area. He was said to be quite a character, a bit of a card, given to japes and stunts. I found this to be true. Joe Plummer, the rep, looked like his reputation, bluff, boisterous, and ruddy, his formidable frame encased in an expensive-looking but slightly seedy suit. "Ed, how the hell are you? Gimme the bag. Jesus Christ it's good to see you again."

Considering we had only met once before, and then only very briefly, I couldn't but feel that he was being overly friendly. But this was the American way. I thought it charming. We walked to the parking place. He stopped at a large Cadillac. Pink it was. Wow. The car's over here. Talk about over the top.

He wheeled out of the airport and swung onto a palm tree-lined boulevard. Ah, this was more like it. This was the way America was supposed to look. Traffic, heavy and fast, swept along in both directions, much of it with the tops down and the drivers in short sleeves. Oh, smell the fumes. Inhale the scent of pleasure, the electricity of the atmosphere. This is the place to be. These are the movements I wanted to dance to.

"Here's the hotel." Joe pulled up to the Beverley Hills Hilton. I knew this was classy, but didn't at the time, know how classy. Joe wanted to take me out, but I excused myself on the grounds of sheer exhaustion. "Tomorrow then. First get some rest. I'll pick you up at nine in the lobby." I checked in and was escorted to the room, which was, without exception, the most palatial I had seen. The company did not scrimp when it came to travel arrangements.

I ordered room service. A double martini, salad, filet mignon with baked potato, and apple a la mode. While I was waiting I switched on the television. Colour. Unusual in the early sixties. I clicked idly through news programs, family sitcoms. It was six or seven o'clock when, 'What's this?' An elliptical banked track, figures in shiny tight suits, helmets, boots and roller skates hurtling around, rattling and crashing into each other, fans on their feet screaming abuse and encouragement, fighting amongst themselves. The noise was overpowering. The scene resembling a Babylonian orgy with cola, popcorn, French fries and mustard-soaked bread, and meat instead of vinous filled goblets and delicacies of ox tongue and artichokes being gobbled and spilt.

Then the women gladiators appeared. Young, obviously this was a youthful sport, attractive and well-built, curvaceous but tough. The crowds had their favourites and greeted them with salutes of their name repeated over and over. The girls, with teeth gritted and faces set like masks, tripped each other with venomous shrieks and rabbit punches to necks and shoulders.

It was a spectacle that would have been relished by

the jaded of Rome seated in the Coliseum. I could make no sense of the rules or the point of this unseemly and chaotic fracas and was about to turn off when the door was tapped and dinner was served. Early it was when I doused lights, drew curtains, and opened windows. The sound of the city many floors below was stirring and exciting and lulled me to my sleep.

After breakfast, which was buffet and substantial, I met Joe and we set off to visit all the stores with which he was familiar. He introduced me to the sales and design people, who proceeded to tell me of the styles and colours their customers preferred in their furnishings. It was interesting how tastes altered from east to west and north to south, both in wood case goods and in upholstered items. I took notes and promised due attention. They were convivial and charming, spoke of England with pleasure, and wished me well in my endeavours.

It was evening. Cool, with the sun descending, its afterglow casting a roseate glow over the tall towers of downtown Los Angeles. It reminded me very much of the Mediterranean littoral. We could be in Cannes or Palermo or Alexandria. There was that feeling that the sea was just over the horizon. The smell was of money and of good living, frangipani, veiled entrances of sidewalk cafés which clinked and chattered and vented perfumes, tobacco, and cooked spices out to the sidewalk.

One of these we entered. Joe was obviously well

known and we were seated at once. Drinks appeared and I looked around. All the drinkers and diners were, without exception, beautiful and engaged in intensive and serious conversation. "They're mostly film people," Joe remarked. I looked with more interest. "Mike Wilding," said Joe casually. "Just split with Elizabeth Taylor,"

As discreetly as possible, I glanced at a very tanned, slightly built man in a light linen suit. He was grinning broadly at something someone was saying and did not seem a bit unhappy at the reported domestic trials Joe had just described.

We finished our dinner and after settling the bill, which Joe picked up, left the café. 'okay,' said Joe, "Tighten your seat belt, we're going on the town." We swooped down the freeway into the city. Familiar street names flew by as in a dream. Sunset Boulevard. Signs pointing to Glendale, Santa Monica, Pomona, and all thc othcr namcs that dreams are made of. Malibu, Torrance, half-formed pictures appeared in my mind, none of them accurate probably, but not important. This was where Hollywood was and that was enough for me.

We pulled into a busy and crowded parking lot, bathed in incandescence and neon. "Here we are. The Pink Pussycat," said Joe. He handed the key to an attendant and we proceeded to the flashing lights and pulsating music. Inside it was all lights and life. Tables filled an enormous room, a stage at one end, on which a well-undressed chorus was cavorting, waitresses in outfits of some immodesty attended to the throng of what looked like tourists.

A young woman who looked all of sixteen sat us down. "Oh," she said, "You're English. Oh that's so swell. I'll introduce you to Mr. Wilding." She turned to the nearby table and said "Mr. Wilding, here's a fellow Brit." This was too extraordinary.

"Oh how d'ye do?" he said, very white teeth, very handsome, very tight.

"Er, how d'ye do?" I replied, very impressed and very sober. He was with friends, two women and another man. Introductions, which I didn't hear, were made, and some brief conversation ensued. We toasted old England and turned to the disrobing on the stage. After an hour or so, we left and did a bar crawl through various parts of the town. What fun we had and what a price was paid next day.

I spent a few more days working with Joe and then got on a plane to go to the city by the bay.

A girl friend from Wisconsin days lived in town and met me at the airport. She deposited me at the Mark Hopkins and we arranged to meet next day for breakfast at the restaurant on top of the hotel. Now I always knew that

I was uncomfortable with heights. What I didn't know was that when we met next day we were to climb to the top of the skyscraper by an outside glass elevator, the configuration of which was such as to keep this fact from the rider until the whole contraption was speeding to its destination.

Ascending above lower structures with giddying effect, the fact that some child in front of me was banging on the glass and screaming didn't make me feel any more secure. The last few hundred feet rocketed by with my eyes shut. A smooth stop and the sound of doors opening alerted me to turn and stumble onto terra firma. "My God Teddy, you're as white as a sheet."

"I hate heights. I should have told you. There had better be another way down, otherwise I'm here for ever." There was some laughter, but as far as I was concerned, there was little humour in it. To pile one thing on another, the restaurant proper was revolving. This was altogether too much.

I tried to eat my Eggs Benedict and ignore the city moving by far below, but to no avail. I heard myself plaintively asking for relief. "Can we go down now?" She was a kind girl, quickly called for the bill, and stood up. She helped me totter out of the room and, thank heavens, to an inside elevator. We descended in walled security. I spent the best part of the day in my room.

That evening I was to meet some friends I had

made when in Majorca, actually at the same time that I met Laura. They had a shop in town that sold children's toys and nursery stuff and I had got rather fond of them.

Promptly at six we met in the lobby. Their names were Herrmann, Birdy, and Tom. It was marvelous to see them again. They were vivacious and full of beans. "Teddy, come on. The car's parked illegally outside. We're going somewhere special for dinner. Some very rich friends of ours asked us out and we said we should bring you and they said terrific."

Oh, forget anything I said that was critical of this country and its people. It's wonderful and they are wonderful. Top down, a white and shiny convertible being eyed by the doorman waited, emolument took place, and with much saluting and bowing, we were wished well on our way.

We yelled at each other to be heard above the canyons of traffic in this most perpendicular of cities that seemed so fragile yet so enduring. Where L.A. had excited me by its immediacy and brazen unashamed commercialism, San Francisco appealed, first by its sheer architectural beauty, situation, and historical associations, but as well, in a subtler less obvious way. This place had secrets, hidden and forbidden.

We had reached the restaurant, and were walking towards the door, Birdy chattering as we went, Tom leading the way. Birdy was describing the people we were to meet, who had lots of lolly. Apparently the wife was the one with the cash, daughter of one of the great railway barons, but still nice. He was just as nice. Their names were Julia and Bob. In we went to be immediately divested of hats and coats by a pretty check girl who gave me the eye and escorted us to our table, already occupied by two people.

The man got up smiling. Introductions were made, and first impressions were formed. He was young looking and very good-looking, she, older and plainer, both extremely cordial. martinis were ordered. This looked like a convivial evening. I looked at the menu. "Alexis," it said. I've since been told, probably the best restaurant in the city. It did turn out to be one of the most enjoyable evenings of my life.

We were to go sailing next day, a Sunday, in their boat across the bay at a place called Sausalito. The night ended up with me picking up the hatcheck girl and inviting her along next day.

The day came too early, with my wake up call squeaking in my ear. I took a quick shower and dressed. I had nothing to wear for small boat sailing, which is what I expected to be doing. They had told me that casual was the rig, so I left tie off, and went to the lobby. They were all there, less my new friend. We were to pick her up on the way.

It was a lovely shiny sparkling morning. I was discomfited to see that they were all in very smart outfits of worn jeans, tee shirts and running shoes. Birdy even had a blue and white dotted scarf around her neck. I felt quite over-dressed.

The girl was waiting outside her apartment building. She was even more over-dressed than me and even had high heels on. "Oh lord this is not good, a little black dress for a sail?" Oh well. She was gorgeous. Her name was Miranda. No one else seemed put out by her appearance, indicating to me once more the lack of silly rules and prejudices that existed here compared to England.

We were now driving over the bridge, the island of the prison way down on our right. Tom went into gory but funny details. We laughed, but looked away. Soon we were winding down a green hill towards the sea, surrounded by high hills all about, and then into a large land-locked bay with wooden jetties, alongside of which were scores of boats of every type and size.

I turned to Tom who was helping unload boxes of food and drink from the car. "Here you go Teddy." He passed me a large carton of Canada Dry Tonic. "Follow Bob and the girls." I did, half walking half stumbling, with my head down looking at my feet in their shiny black leather shoes. Quelle embarasse. The wet greasy wood dock caused great care and attention on my part. I heard sounds of greeting and noises of heavy engines being started up, heavy and powerful marine engines. Withal, I looked up to see a high hull stretching forever in either direction. It was a major motor launch, complete with a small exhaust funnel, radar and mast, also a crew, who were helping us climb a companionway that slanted up the side. Perhaps Miranda had worn the appropriate outfit after all.

After an extensive tour of the boat, including an inspection of the gleaming, spotless, engine room, we repaired to the main saloon where a table laid for lunch awaited. Two Filipino stewards seated us and the meal proceeded, accompanied by some very fine Californian white wines. As we were having coffee the boat started to tremble and the sound of engines that had been running at low RPMs, became stronger. We began to move. We all put our cups down and made for the upper deck.

We were indeed on the move, heading for the open bay, picking up speed. Ahead, the massive, impressive, bridge crowded with tiny cars. It was mid-afternoon. The day was warm. My mood was content. I sat in a deck chair and puffed happily on a cigar that Bob had produced. I noticed Miranda was smoking one too. She looked rather elegant.

We passed a few cargo ships heading into the dock area and passed under the bridge. A surreal experience, which I was still savouring, when suddenly, just ahead and to our left side, a submarine surfaced, water streaming from her hull. She wasn't moving and just lay there rocking gently, and looking menacing, and, when she hooted, sounding threatening. The crew appeared. An ensign was raised, which, as she got under way, began to snap bravely in the air. It was a sight to stir one's blood for sure. We waved and were saluted.

We continued until it started to get a little dark, at which point we passed another launch similar to ours, with much yelling, waving and other salutations. It seemed this was Julia's brother's boat, a twin to ours. There was a lot of money in this family.

The rest of the evening consisted of more cocktails, then dinner, then it was agreed it was time to head for our respective beds. I had concluded that the hatcheck girl was not interested. She had thought I had money, and when she found out I was just a working stiff, albeit with good connections, rapidly got a headache. The result was that I got a good night's sleep, needed badly, as early next day, it was back to the Carolinas and the real world.

Spring came and went. Work continued interesting, but tiring and stressful. My social life got better and better. With more new friends, having a flat, a sports car, and an English accent, my reputation had entered into the unofficial register of the University of NC Women's College as a pretty good date. Good for a meal, a few drinks, and someone who gave good parties and didn't fumble unpleasantly or inappropriately on the first dates. So, all in all, life was good.

I met another of those people who had throughout my life affected the general direction I was taking and who influenced me for good or ill. His name was George de la Fortescue, known locally as "Dealer Fortescue." He was a devastatingly handsome, tall, bearded, out-of-work actor and serious drinker. He was probably one of the most generous, compassionate men I have ever met. We became very fond of each other and were to spend many memorable times together.

He was knowledgeable, humorous, loved the girls and had the manners of a Romanov duke, which is what he looked like. He owned an old '41 Packard car, which we would drive into the women's college grounds to pick up our dates. The combination of this massive black limousine and the handsome driver was enough, I think, to have made many the female student heart flutter on occasion.

He introduced me to a rather marvelous group of friends: actors, artists, academics, and writers. We would gather Sunday afternoons to drink and set the world right. George never was, while I knew him, successful in getting back on the stage, so got a temporary job of being a locomotive fireman with the Southern Railroad in Winston Salem. A most unlikely job for one so sensitive. But oddly enough he really enjoyed himself and made a lot of friends amongst the railroad fraternity. Sadly, the drink finally brought him down and a promising talent was wasted and lost to the world at the bottom of a ravine, where his car took him after control was lost on a night of impenetrable fog. I miss him still.

* * * *

It was about this time that I met Vianne. She told me, after we were married, that she had seen me taking my laundry to the cleaners, had remarked the car, and had thought me not bad looking.

Vianne and the Morgan

She engineered a meeting and that was that. She was very cute and very young, loved all things English, was highly intelligent, and she completely enchanted me. We dated and became lovers.

I met her parents who lived in the mountains. Mama was an ex-teacher, bright as a bird, gentle but tough, with a no-nonsense attitude that was refreshing. Dad was ex-USMC, a drill sergeant with a formidable bark and a heart of gold. He was as deaf as a post, so that when I wanted to hear about his trials in the war in the Pacific, he would invariably misunderstand and would ramble on about some other subject apropos of nothing. But what a darling man. They took me to their hearts.

Then the letter arrived. Laura said she missed me. She had rented a cottage in Provincetown, Massachusetts for a week. Could I come and share it with her and some other model friends? This was, to say the least, awkward. I really wanted to see her, and at that time the relationship with Vianne was still in early stages, fairly tentative.

So, off I went, ostensibly for business, feeling slightly guilty. But, by the time I got to Provincetown and had seen her and the cottage, I had managed to rationalize all difficulties and unease into the background. Laura had two girl friends sharing with her. It was a tiny little house. My room was in the attic and I was introduced as a gay designer friend. We had five crazy days of sun, wine, and food. At the end of the last day one of the girls said,

"You're not gay, are you Teddy?" We left each other, still caring for each other, but knowing too, that our paths were unlikely to cross again.

⁕ ⁕ ⁕ ⁕

Back in Greensboro I returned to my work and to life that was generally amenable. I had a new little house that I rented. It was built like a small Beau Geste fort, stucco on brick with one gigantic room that had thirty-two foot ceilings, a large open fireplace at one end, and a mezzanine floor with minstrel gallery at the other.

Vianne and I in Greensboro

These floors connected by a staircase, the upper containing two bedrooms and a bathroom. The main floor had a kitchen tucked in underneath the stairs. The main room also boasted two wide windows, one on each side that reached almost to the ceiling. The resulting effect was one of space and grandeur. I furnished it in what I liked to think was eclectic sparseness, and proceeded to give some quite startlingly good parties.

Some of the most memorable parties were arranged about the times of the two annual furniture markets. These were held in the nearby city of High Point and brought people from all over the world. I used to invite all the designers I knew and all the best customers we had, together with some we were after, and, having now the connections I had at the women's college of UNC, I would invite all the students who liked to party, to join us. There would be lashings of food and drink; everyone dressed to the nines, a small band, and servants. These celebratory occasions became well-known and invitations were sought after with enthusiasm. They also helped create a lot of new business, so were paid for by the company.

I was seeing more and more of Vianne now and we were becoming closer in every way. She was spending every weekend with me and was becoming indispensable.

We decided to marry. Mum and Dad both approved. We all liked each other very much. It would be quiet, a few friends, and in a registry office, no fuss of any sort. It was high June. The official ceremony was brief. The party afterwards was hectic, overflowing with people, some of whom were unknown to me, and going on for hours after we had left to stay at a hotel on our way to the mountains to visit her parents.

Later in the year, Vianne informed me that we were to have a baby, due some time next spring. She of course was delighted. I was not so sure. Everything was suddenly becoming overwhelming. I was in my mid-thirties, she just out of her teens. From confirmed bachelor to domestic bliss in such a short time. 'Were we going too fast?'

We were happy though, and her cooking was quite delectable, especially after the last few years of fast fried food, too many late nights, and overindulgence in both alcohol and tobacco. I certainly felt better since eating balanced meals, was sleeping better and generally was slowing down in the party department. My work was less stressful, partly because I had someone to share frustrations with.

Later, at a sales convention, the president of the company told me that although they were reasonably pleased with my performance, my state of singleness had given them some anxiety and displeasure. Vianne's appearance on the scene had reassured them as to my dependability and permanence. The fact that she was young, cute, and bright did not go amiss.

* * * *

Autumn and winter came and went. I was now as eager as could be in anticipation of the coming event, and when the time came, was as nervous, clumsy, and useless as most fathers-to-be are. Poor Vianne had a rough time before, during, and after the delivery, but all was well. When I first saw them, they were doing all the right things. The father, on the other hand, was in a state of shock and took to his bed for a time.

I adored Vicky and I think she liked me. We would gaze at each other while she gripped my fingers and gurgled. I was good at the lighter moments of parenthood but not so brilliant when it came to the more realistic parts. Thankfully, Vianne had been brought up as a Southern Girl, which included the expectation of domestic responsibilities being largely borne by themselves. Thus it was in the sixties, especially in the South. I am forever grateful that I was born when I was. Today, I would have been hung on the nearest lamppost. I am, however, aware of my shortcomings and ask forgiveness.

* * * *

Not long after Vicky's arrival, I was approached by an association that lobbied for the increased use of oak in furniture. They were planning a trip to England to see if they could get the Brits to look at oak as a fashion veneer instead of the more common cherry, mahogany, and walnut. They were to put on a big show at the Hilton hotel in London and were taking a well-known designer, who I knew well, some wood production people, and I would go along to give a talk about the ease and potential of finishing the wood in a glamorous way.

I jumped at the chance. I was allowed to take Vianne and all expenses would be paid. We arranged for the grandparents to look after Vicky, bought some new clothes, alerted my family, and jumped on a plane. It would be one of the best of all trips. Showing Vianne London and introducing London and my family to my new American bride was for me a highlight of the trip. They all adored her and the feelings were mutual.

I gave my talk, which went over reasonably well. The hall was packed with fashion journalists, designers, and manufacturers. Some of them, I'm sure, were there for the free bar, but I think it was a success. We all went to a pub in Mayfair after and got hammered. One of the designers made a pass at Vianne. I'd forgotten how pushy some Brits could be in such circumstances. She was rather flattered though.

The next few days we spent touring factories and showrooms and generally touting the wood specie around the UK. We were then free to spend the next two weeks as we liked.

❋ ❋ ❋ ❋

We went down to Dorset to visit my favourite uncle. This was Lovell, my dad's brother. He had a small dairy farm near Dorchester in the middle of Hardy country. We went by train.

Lovell, Vianne, Edward, Anne, Simon and Djemila at Dorset

The engine in front was still driven by steam and was quite beautiful. Great Western Green, probably built in the thirties or forties but still in good shape, her paintwork and shiny turned-steel parts coated thinly with oil. She had that patina that comes from sunshine reflecting from a perfectly smooth surface.

Clanking and snorting she entered the cavernous station. A brief glimpse of driver and fireman, white teeth flashing through the coal dust, grinning with pride at all the attention, black oilcloth caps down tight on their faces, then, creaking and groaning, the whole train came to a halt and doors began to open, slamming all the way down the line.

We had decided to go first class and were sitting back gazing at the backs of the little houses of south London, rattling over the points of the complicated track system criss-crossing from one line to another, passing goods, trains, and local traffic until the train seemed to stretch itself to get into its long distance pace with that peculiar and nostalgic clickety-click staccato of the English train.

"Would you like tea sir?" a white-uniformed steward asked, peering through the sliding door.

I always think the Great West Railway the most romantic and exciting of the British train systems. Today it's all British Rail, but we were running on old GWR tracks. The GWR was the line of Sherlock Holmes on his way to deal with the Baskerville case. It conjured up visions of peaty dark moors on moonless nights with gloomy rambling houses that had only one light on, suggesting sinister activities underway. It also led to seaports like Bristol and the Welsh harbours, where one embarked on freighters leaving at tide's-turn for the Americas, or the dangers and delights of African adventures.

It started to get, not dark, but that wonderful late afternoon pearl-like light that comes when the sun casts its afterglow. We were coming into Dorchester station where we were to be met by my uncle. I lowered the window and looked out. There was a considerable crowd on the platform. I couldn't see him anywhere. We got down and a porter picked up the bags.

"Teddy," I heard in Lovell's unmistakable voice. Tall, smiling with pleasure, here he was, bearing down on us, people just getting out of the way. He hugged me and turned to Vianne. "My darling Vianne," he pronounced it Veeahn. "You must be exhausted." He hugged her too and led the way, with long athletic strides, to a crimson 3.8 Jaguar parked in the lot with two dogs in the back, a little Dachshund called Max and a big Bulldog with the predictable name of Winston.

"Veeahn, you sit with me. Teddy, you're with the dogs," he chortled and winked at Vi. Lovell was probably about sixty-five, but looked and behaved like forty-five. He was my father's younger brother and had escaped the horrors of the trenches in the first war by just a couple of years. He was universally adored in the family, had had a full and exciting life, much of which had been spent in the Middle East, primarily in the oil business with Shell.

His WWII years were in the western desert and Egypt. He had been returning to England in '39 to join his regiment, a lowly lieutenant, when he met, in the bar at Shepherd's Hotel, an old friend who said, "Don't do that, take over the Military Police here instead." He was immediately gazetted as lieutenant colonel and preceeded to take on the extremely difficult and complex task of engaging the Italians in battle and the Australian army in the fleshpots of Cairo, the latter, he said, giving him the most trouble.

We were now humming down the highway, doing, I noticed, about ninety. Vi didn't seem too worried. The dogs slobbered, Lovell kept up a running commentary. The beauty of the passing countryside transfixed me. This was my first trip to England since 1953 when I had gone to the Sudan.

I had forgotten the green, the almost incandescent green. I hadn't thought about the heavy, high-looming hedgerows of the west country, the ivy, the hornbeam, the winding lanes and the new worlds at every turn, the village and the inn and the pious church and soldier statue with the long list of names, so English, so far away in time and space, and where they lay, so sad and so foreign, Ypres, Paschendaale and the Somme, Zonnebeek, Vimy and Arras. I heard Lovell's hilarious comments, only partly listening. I was really getting choked up. It had been so long. It had been too long.

We turned off the road and went up a drive to a large whitewashed cottage. This was Lower Rew Farm. I had been there before, just after the war, and had loved it then. Out came Anne and Mila, my cousin. Kitty, Lovell's daughter with Anne followed behind. Djemila was Lovell's child with his first wife, Tanetta, and had been born in Jerusalem. She was my favourite. Everyone hugged and kissed. The dogs ran around in circles. A young man appeared and was introduced. He was Anne's boy, Simon, from a previous marriage. Then the laughter began, not ending until we left.

The house was quite old and full of character. The stairs to the bedroom were almost perpendicular, the steps narrow, so that one adopted a sideways position to ascend. Anne showed us our room, along a corridor low and beamed, up a step, down a step, the scent of wax and flowers, a right turn, and down two steps into a room with a small but deep window which looked out to a sheep-cropped field, the view beyond to misty hills crowned with trees, the sound of magpies settling in for the night. I was close to tears. Vianne was enchanted. We sat on the beds and chattered. After washing hands, we went down to join the others. "What do you drink usually?" asked Lovell. "martinis? Good God, aren't they rather dangerous?"

I noticed that everyone else was drinking scotch or beer, but I had brought a bottle of gin so didn't mind repeating the request.

"Not really. We always put ice in ours so they are quite innocuous."

"Oh really," said Lovell in his lovely Edwardian accent and with a droll look on his face. "Well I think, Teddy, that that's a lot of what they use in tennis, and I don't mean racquets."

Everyone was talking a mile a minute. We drank and ate cheese straws. People rushed to the kitchen and back. At everyone's request, Vianne sang a cowboy song and put on a very exaggerated southern accent. They thought it delightful. We had a salad and a marvelous soufflé followed by homemade apple pie smothered in clotted cream, then coffee and brandy. We sat up talking, until the eyes closed with sheer exhaustion and we were forced, reluctantly, to go to bed.

I faded into sleep marveling at the silence of the night, and didn't wake until dawn. I got up and crept to the open window and looked out. Incandescently green. A light mist lay over all. Below me a small neat garden with hollyhocks and delphiniums looming above a tangle of smaller flower plantings. I hugged myself. I was really home.

Everyone was up early for breakfast, which was old-fashioned and thoroughly English: eggs, bacon, fried bread, grilled tomatoes, and scads of toast and marmalade, one jar of which, Lovell had made himself and was very proud of, saying, "Now this marmalade was made by Mrs. Tosspot down the road," pointing to another jar on the table with a shrug at its dubious quality. "On the other hand, this one made by myself is quite superior." This with a twinkle in his eye.

"You really are full of shit," drawled Anne. He chuckled. We adored him.

The coffee was served French style, au lait, with milk straight from the cow. The farm was a dairy operation. The cows were, I believe, either Gurnseys or Jerseys. Lovell had given them all the names of female relatives, dead or alive. The one that was difficult, in a milk production sense, was named Constance, after our detested step-grandmother. After eating, Lovell showed us around the rest of the house and grounds, then up the hill to meet the herd. The dairy was on top of the hill and the house tucked into the side, cozy and protected from the winds that blew from the north.

One day I was sitting in the library leafing through the collection of military volumes Lovell had collected, when there was a banging on the front door. I heard Anne go to answer. There was a low conversation, then a pause. "Lovell," she shouted. He was in the kitchen chopping something up. "There's a man here come to paint the barn roof." Pause.

"Tell him to fuck off," Lovell shouted back. More low talk at the door.

"Lovell, he says he'll throw in the drive shed too for no extra charge."

"Ahh, come in dear boy," said Lovell striding to the door, chuckling and looking at me to share the joke.

In the sitting room, which was comfortably furnished in that natural way so beloved of the interior decorator, but that has to be real to be successful, I noticed on the wall, a shadow box containing three military decorations. I recognized, with awe, the Victoria Cross, the Distinguished Service Order, and the Military Cross, the three most prestigious awards that can be won for valour in the field. The last two bore insignia showing they had been awarded twice. They belonged to Anne's father who had won them in the First World War, the VC posthumously, which was often the case. One had to virtually die to get it.

Anne had been in the Middle East serving with the army when she met Lovell and they had fallen in love. She had spent an interesting, and probably risky, part in army wireless intelligence and counter-espionage. I never knew her to talk about it and only learnt about her involvement after her death. Apparently she was employed by MI-6 in an operation with the name of "Cheese." She played the role of a Greek girl friend of a fictitious renegade Russian called Nicosoff (the Brits do like their little jokes) who hated the British and pretended to relay information to the Germans in the western desert. Anne's codename was "Misanthrope." The Germans were entirely taken in by the subterfuge and continued to believe the false intelligence they were fed.

Night after night she would be dropped off at some remote point in the desert with her suitcase radio, which she would use to make contact with her German opposite number and exchange information, hers faulty, theirs correct. Operation Cheese. It was reported to have played an important part in the deception plan leading to success at the battle of Alamein. The novel, "The English Patient" makes much of the veil of deceit that occurred at that time in the real world. With a bit of prodding, she would, very occasionally, tell the story of the night someone tried to get into her room in the night. She always slept with a little Beretta pistol under her pillow. Waking, she calmly shot the intruder and promptly went back to sleep.

Her family was from Ulster, birthplace of so many gallant soldiers, some of whom were very senior, including Montgomery, Alanbrooke, Wellington of course, and Alexander. She was reserved, but close and loving with those she cared for. We liked each other at once. I see her now, preparing dinner, a glass of wine in one hand as she stirred some delectable stew in an enormous cast iron pot, smoke climbing from the green Aga stove, which, besides cooking the food, also heated the house and always had a kettle on the hob for the quick cup of tea, puffing, rather inappropriately, on a cigarette, and carrying on a conversation with Lovell two rooms away. God, I loved them.

She said to me, one day as we were driving around the countryside seeing sights, "Teddy, you're interested in Lawrence of Arabia aren't you?" I answered in the affirmative. "Would you like to see his grave?"

"Indeed I would." She drove on, and coming to a fork in the road, paused, then turned down an even narrower lane that was overhung with ivy and mistletoe draped on oak branches. A little church, very grey and silent appeared. We stopped and got out. There was no one about. Through a gate and along a paved path with ancient memorial stones, broken statuary, mossy and lichened, this was an old place of burial. We came to a hedge lined with stones. Newer, more recent, some with wilted flowers, but mostly forgotten and forlorn.

One was inscribed T.E. Lawrence, Fellow of All Souls College Oxford. R.I.P. That's all. So modest, so obscure. Next to his grave, one that said, Flight Sergeant so and so, RAF, shot down over Dortmund Germany, 1942. Behind the hedge, black and white Friesian cows chewed contentedly.

I knew that we had some obscure relationship with the Lawrence of Arabia story and got more out of Lovell that evening over drinks. It seems that his first wife, my aunt Tanetta, whose American family had settled in the Holy Land before the First World War, had, while they were running their American hospital in Jerusalem, met Colonel Lawrence as he was winding up the desert campaign when he had raised the tribal Bedouin against the Turks. There are, I believe, artifacts in the Imperial War Museum in London that attest to this connection, and, I am told, accounts of how my second cousin by marriage, introduced Lawrence to Lowell Thomas, the American correspondent who was instrumental in making the name Lawrence, famous with the movie "Revolt in the Desert."

The days passed much too quickly. Inevitably the visit was coming to an end. We had other family to see, including my father, stepmother, and half-sister Antonia, who I had last seen when very little, and as a baby sitter. Tearful and extended goodbyes took place. That awful feeling one has when retracing one's steps after a happy period overcame me and the trip back to London was gloomy. Vi was sad. They had been so sweet to her and were delighted that she was now part of the family.

❋ ❋ ❋ ❋

We spent a couple of days in town. The visit to

Ramsgate to see my father had been delayed for some family reason that escapes me, but now we were on the way. I was a little apprehensive. Dad could be charming and lovable, but he was changeable and was often irascible and in drink could be quite unpleasant.

The village where we were staying, Bearstead, in Kent, was reached, and we dismounted from the coach. The platform was deserted. The place was just a small halt. In no time the train pulled out and disappeared from view. We looked around. There was not a soul to be seen and not a building anywhere around. It began to rain. We ran to shelter in a tiny little corrugated roofed shelter and huddled disconsolately together. The rain streamed down. It was starting to get dark. 'What the hell do I do now?'

Vi was, thank God, no shrinking violet, not much fazed her, but this was pretty bad. We were tired, hungry, and starting to get wet. It was chilly for June, typically English summer weather. At that moment I heard the sweet sound of a car's engine. Peering out, I saw a beat up old Land Rover bouncing up the lane. I rushed out and waved. It came to a stop. I noticed it had milk churns in the back. Out came a burly, bearded man, our saviour, I hoped. He saw our state and motioned us inside. He was marvelous. He picked up our bags and threw them in the back. We sat in the warm, beautifully smelly, muddy, straw-strewn front seats, the engine throbbing. I lit a cigarette.

We were relieved.

He unloaded the churns and got back in. The car door was slammed shut and we were away, rocketing down the bumpy lane, the little wipers flicking back and forth. Not a word had been said. "There's only one taxi in the village. You chose the day to arrive when it's on the blink, If it wasn't for my having to drop off the churns for the early milk train, you'd have had an uncomfortable night." We thanked him profusely and explained our reasons for being here.

My stepmother, of whom I was very fond, lived near the village in a tiny cottage and we had rooms at an inn in the village for the night while we visited her. Our driver nodded and continued driving in silence. In a short time we were at the pub and he helped us unload. I asked how I could thank him and he said I could buy him a pint in the bar later.

The place was fantastic, a cliché of ye olde English hostelry, but of course absolutely genuine, low-beamed ceilings, a patina of tobacco coating the walls and ceilings, horse brasses, dark paintings, the smell of good old English ale, and something roasted being prepared. The sound of laughter, conversation and glasses clinking together, came from the bar.

We went to our room and rested, bathed. No showers here. We dressed and went downstairs. In the bar the eyes all swiveled round to look at Vi. We saw the man who had rescued us earlier. He introduced us around. The first thing I had to do, after ordering a round, was to call Connie, my step-mother, to have her join us for drinks and dinner. I reached her quickly, and she arrived in minutes.

Connie had, at this time, left my father, and was living alone in the gatehouse of a large manor near the village. I think she had some arrangement that gave her free lodgings in exchange for companionship for the old lady who owned and lived in the main house. Cecil, my father, was living in a room in a hotel in Ramsgate, one of those separate tables sort of establishments, all retired Indian army officers, gin and tonics, unpaid bills, and wicker chairs. We were to see him tomorrow. We were also hoping to see Antonia.

We had a great evening, drinking that marvelous English beer called "Bitter," telling jokes, and talking a mile a minute, the main subject being my dad's bad habits, and what she had had to put up with that finally forced her to abandon ship.

Up next day at what my friend George Price used to call "sparrows fart," we got a hire-car from a local garage and drove over to Connie's. It was a sweet little cottage, roses round the door, a well-kept gravel drive leading up a slight rise through some trees to an imposing red brick mansion in the style of the Tudor period. I was told later that it had been built for one of Henry VIII's numerous girl friends.

We sat in the cozy sitting room and had coffee.

Connie told us some stories that were fascinating, about the little house. Apparently it had been used by the SOE (Special Operations Executive) during the war as a last stop for operatives being landed in France to work with the underground and Maquis Resistance. She showed us her bedroom, which had been the final checkroom for last instructions and inspections of equipment and personal possessions. It wouldn't do to be found to have a London bus ticket on you when being searched by the Gestapo.

The individuals would then be helped through the window onto a rough lawn and through a gated hedge to a waiting Westland Lysander, its engines ticking over, the moonlight casting long shadows over the meadow. For some men and women, this would be the last they would see of England. I knew that Connie had been in the American Red Cross during the war. I suspect her duties were more onerous than just bandaging wounds.

Just before lunchtime we set off for Ramsgate to find Dad. Connie didn't come. When we got there, we went straight to the hotel. It was a typical English seaside establishment called the Foy Boat. These are semi-private places with long-term guests. The hall was cool and dark after the bright sunshine outside. I had to adjust for a second to be able to see. There was no one behind the desk. We turned to the staircase to see a little bird-like woman tripping down the stairs. "Can I help you?" she chirped.

"I'm looking for my father, Major Payne."

"Major Payne?" she repeated. "Major Payne? Oh you mean Cecil. Oh he's down at the Cricketers' Arms. Let's see, no, it's already noon, he'll have gone to the Freemasons by now." It seemed that Dad had a daily routine and some order in his peregrinations. Off we went in search.

Finally we found him at about two that afternoon. He was standing at the bar, one foot up on the brass rail, holding forth to an admiring and attentive group of drinkers. He looked round at us, all six foot five of him, still a quite an impressive figure, straight and soldierly. "My dear Teddy. And this is Vianne. My dear, what will you have?" Vi melted. He still had the charm.

We met the others. They were all regulars and knew each other well. My father was obviously well-liked. He could tell a good story, and seemed pleased when I told a couple of jokes, pleased and, I think, surprised. This was the day, I believe, that I lost the inferiority complex I always had before when around Dad. Later that night, in bed, Vi said, "Your father is wonderful. How could you have been frightened of him?"

"I can't think," I answered.

We all met next day for lunch, at which we were to meet Antonia, my half sister. She arrived and quickly became the centre of attention. She was very affectionate with Cecil who obviously adored her. I felt slightly envious at the way she behaved with him. They were both so comfy with each other. I kept seeing him in lights that had never lit when Madeleine and I were children. He had always been so stern and disapproving then, so angry and foreboding. He had been a frustrated, bitter, and reluctant parent. Now he was at ease, contented, the paterfamilias in situ. When she was impertinent with him and he laughed at the tease, I really hurt. I thanked God my sister hadn't been present. She would never have recognized him for the same cold, unfeeling man she had known as a small girl.

I forgot my momentary feelings of regret however, and determined to enjoy this new and improved version of Dad. We all had a great time and I was able to spend a little while alone with him. He was so nice to be with, no critical comments, no sarcastic jabs. I began to wonder if I had imagined the past, its tears and confused unhappiness. We talked as equals and spoke of him joining us in America, though why I brought that up I'll never know. He would have hated the States. The one thing we didn't discuss was the past. It might never have happened.

❋ ❋ ❋ ❋

It was time to leave. We had to go on to see other relatives and then return, reluctantly, to America. I really wished I could stay in England, having rediscovered my family. The thought of being so far away again rankled. Perhaps one day we could return for good. The States had been good to me, but I was still emotionally attached to England in so many ways. Vi would have been happy to move and Vicky would love it

We saw my last major family connection. This was my aunt Zoe. She was my Dad's sister, a great beauty in her time and still attractive, elegant, and graceful. She had married a naval officer in the twenties and had spent some years with him traveling the world, following the various ships he had commanded. He was now a gruff old sea dog with the retired rank of Commodore. They lived in comfort in a small family hotel in Woking. He and I had always got on and she was an absolute darling.

They both lavished much attention on Vi. The first meeting had been a bit tricky though. We had first met Zoe in the bar, and she warned us that he had just given up smoking the day before, and was consequentially in a grumpy mood. At that moment enter Uncle Kenneth, unfortunately, just as Vi, not seeing him, lit up.

"Oh Ken," gushed Zoe, "Come and meet Teddy's lovely wife, Vianne."

He glared at her and the newly lit cig and growled, "I see you have that filthy smoking habit. How are you Teddy?"

"Now, now, Kenneth," said Zoe embarrassedly,

"Shall we have a drink?" She looked around vaguely.

After a couple of pink gins had gone down, he became positively boyish with Vi and flirted unashamedly. She lapped it up and the day was saved. Next morning at breakfast when he showed Vi how to bone a kipper with one small, surgical incision, they were chums for life.

The time finally arrived for us to leave. We had hoped to see two other cousins, Zoe's children, Adrian, who was about my age, and his younger brother, Anthony, both now married with children. But we had to postpone until another time. Now, off to the airport, and soon we were dozing at 30,000 feet over the Atlantic.

Back in the States, I busied myself with being a father, a good husband, and a provider, or at least, I tried. Those were such happy days. I had decided that I liked being married and having a settled domestic life. We had lots of friends and did all the things together that newlyweds do. Love-in-a-cottage was in full flight. We had lots in common, liking and deploring the same foods, people, fashions, movies, colours and manners.

Vi was a marvelous mum. Vicky thrived. We visited family in the mountains and made the odd visit to my sisters in Wisconsin, a long and tiring drive over the mountains, but always more than worth the trouble because we enjoyed being with them all so much.

The memories of all the things that had made England so desirable, faded into oblivion, only brought out and dusted down for embellished anecdotes to tell friends over cocktails. I used to regale them all with stories of the family in England, especially Lovell. They all laughed, except for Madeleine who would look pensive. She had an inordinate fear of flying and had not, and would not, ever return to England. She also suffered from a bad case of inferiority complex in relation to the rest of the family. That had not been helped by Dad's attitude towards her when young.

I was, in many ways, her connection to them and to England in general. She had her own life now with her family and friends, which were numerous and loving. She had a great gift for interior decorating and with Bob's talent for fashioning wood, made several houses and rooms in the area blush with pride. She was funny, generous, excessively loving, and loyal. She loved fashion and had impeccable taste.

Bob, whose antecedents were Norwegian, was unquestionably the finest cabinetmaker I had ever come across. And he adored her, was a great foil for her. He shared all her good qualities, but where she had inherited our mother's Italo-Greek passions, he displayed those characteristics of the North: temperate, modest, cool, and rarely flustered. His was the oil that calmed the troubled domestic seas. He was universally loved and invariably trusted. The fact that he loved to laugh and have the occasional Budweiser made him even more appealing.

With their two children, Michael and Diane, who were attractive, had good manners, and obviously possessed talents that promised success in the future, they made up a well-balanced, contented family unit that was an example, certainly to me, and no doubt to all that met them, of what domestic bliss was all about.

* * * *

The years passed happily. The only shadow on my horizon was the job. It was interesting, but I felt I had done all that was to be done there. I wanted to be somewhere else. It had been 10 years since I moved to the South. It was time to move on. England was the first choice, but so far from Vi's parents as to make it virtually impossible to consider.

One day during the spring furniture market in High Point, I met a young man who worked for a similar company to mine in Canada. We got on very well. He was amusing, unassuming, and English. He described to me the virtues of Canada, not least of which was that it was similar in many ways to England and that there were hordes of Brits living there. He would talk to his boss about me and thought there would be an opening for someone with the experience I had. We left with mutual feelings of approval.

I heard nothing for a while, but then had a phone call from his boss. He wanted to meet me. We arranged a time and place some weeks hence in Louisville Kentucky. In the meantime I was preparing for another trip to England. This time Vicky was going with us.

✻ ✻ ✻ ✻

We left for England from the new Washington Airport, Dulles, and from the moment the wheels left the ground Vicky began to scream. She had started teething. None of the suggested cures helped and the harassed attendants appeared to be giving up when an elderly lady across the aisle said dryly, “Rub some scotch on her gums.” I always carried a flask for emergencies, so quickly unscrewed the cap and did as suggested. The results were miraculous. Vicky licked her lips, smiled, and went to sleep. So did the rest of the plane.

Arriving, slightly hung-over, Vicky included, we got a taxi and headed for London. We were to spend time with

Kitty, my cousin, who was living in Holland Park with husband Rupert, a journalist with The Times, and two children, Pandora and Sebastian. Kitty was doing fantastically interesting and complex work in the field of tapestry and antique carpet repair and was in great demand throughout Britain in all the great houses and museums. Currently she had a contract to work on uniforms in the Imperial War Museum in Lambeth.

We then went down to Kent to see Dad and Connie. Antonia was living in the north and we hoped to see her later. After visiting with Dad we went back to London for a few days. We were then going up to Scotland to stay with Anthony, another cousin who lived somewhere on the east coast at the foot of the highlands. We flew, meaning to land at Inverness, but as it was socked in with fog we were diverted to Edinburgh, where we were to be put on a train to complete the journey. Arriving, we found the festival in full swing.

There were people from all over the world packing into the city. Pandemonium reigned. We managed to get a cab to the station and found our way to the platform where the Flying Scot would shortly be arriving from London. Vicky was behaving like a trooper. Considering everything, we were not doing badly.

The loudspeaker began to send its garbled scarcely understandable message relating to the train's imminent arrival and then with all the majesty that only steam engines could pull off, this famous long distance train pulled in, apple green locomotive and coal tender, followed by teak brown carriages, dining cars, and sleepers. It was then about midnight, so the atmosphere was hushed when we found our carriage.

A little cockney steward picked up the bags and showed us to our sleeping compartment. We were going first class so all sorts of attentions were coming our way. I tipped the steward more than I should have and closed the door. "Is this marvelous or what?" The beds were all made, so after ablutions, we got into the bunks, tired out. There was a tap at the door. It was the steward. He opened the door a crack.

"Would you like tea and biscuits in the morning sir?"

The train began to move and soon we were swaying over the points and crossovers that mark the exits of stations. A feeling of warmth and well-being crept over me. The rhythm of the train settled to a monotonous beat and then suddenly changed to a hollower, deeper note. I sat up. The moonlight was flooding the compartment.

"What is it?" asked Vi.

"Don't know. Hang on." I looked out of the window and my heart stood still. We were crossing the Firth of Forth bridge, the river below glittering in the moon rays, a large ship, lit up, sailing majestically out to sea. Above, the giant girders arced away into the sky. In the distance, the dark mass of the northern shore loomed and beyond that, the highlands of Scotland rose grandly. I lay back, turned on my side and fell asleep.

We got our wake-up call and cup of tea, got sorted out, and headed for the dining car. We ate kippers and brown bread and butter as we gazed at the passing countryside. Actually, the train ran along the coast so the sea was on our right. It was relatively near our destination by the time we had finished eating, so we scampered back to pack and be ready for the imminent arrival.

Anthony was waiting for us at Inverness and very quickly took over logistics from then on. It was a relief to let someone else be the responsible one. I sat in the back of the car with Vicky and lit a cigarette.

We wound up and down steep hills through passes, always mountains in the distance. The views all round were spectacular. The drive took about two hours. By the time we got there, Vicky was fast asleep. Tony had kept Vi amused in front. I was barely awake.

"Here we are."

We pulled into a short gravel drive and stopped. Out of a little cottage came Tony's wife Pauline. She was a dishy blonde with the looks of a film actress. Big hugs and kisses took place. We walked to the door and two little boys appeared accompanied by two Wire-Haired Terriers in full flight. The boys' names were Simon and Timothy. We went inside.

This was an old crofter's cottage dating from before the clearances of the highlands took place, so was of considerable age. The battle of Culloden had taken place somewhere between where we were standing and where we had got off the train, so the land around reeked with history and of extreme violence when the clans clashed with the English army in hand-to-hand combat.

We sat down to lunch and they told us of their life in this magical spot. The property sat with a sea loch in front where Tony could walk down and catch a couple of salmon before breakfast. Behind, the land rose up to a commanding ridge that led to even higher ground, out of sight. Here, Tony would take his shotgun, put a few cartridges in his pocket, and with the dogs, climb the hill into the valley behind and shoot a grouse or pheasant for dinner. This idyllic life and the situation they found themselves in, was due to his job, which was managing a prawn fishing company that lay across the loch near Invergordon.

Pauline was a stay-at-home mum, her hands full with two children, the house, and all sorts of local civic matters in which she was involved. They led a remarkably full social life and, in fact, were taking us to a ball in a nearby castle the next evening. They had told us of the ball before we left the U.S., so I had rented a suit and Vi was all ready with a lovely gown that I was convinced would make her the belle of this ball.

The evening arrived. Vicky was staying with some neighbours with a bunch of other children. We left her lying in a bedroll on the floor of a large room, which she shared with about twenty other kids. She was having the time of her life. Back at the house we were meeting friends of Tony and Pauline's. They were all very elegant, very hunting-and-shooting-and-fishing, and full of good spirits. Some of the men wore the kilt and full regalia and the women had tartan shawls fastened with elaborate brooches to their mostly white dresses. After a few drinks we all set of in a convoy of cars.

It was another lovely, clear, warm, summer night and the rising moon gleamed whitely through the fir trees. The road went through large standing areas of forestry-control estates then across a sprawling, gaunt, and close cropped moor, down a little valley, and there in the distance, on a low rise, looking like a fairy castle floodlit against the night sky, stood a massive pile of crenellated granite beaming with lights. This was the home of a ducal family whose name escapes me

By the time we arrived at the front door, a massive slab of wood bound with great rods of iron and studded with shining rivets with heads like mushrooms, crowds of people were milling about having their invitations checked and cloaks and coats taken into a room set off the hall. The noise and colour, the gowns and uniforms, the tartans of every description were beyond description. I was dying to get to the bar, get a drink and sit back and take it all in. This was one of those moments to relish,

We finally were shown our table, which was right on the dance floor, the perfect position. We were in a grand ballroom, glass French doors at both ends, chandeliers lining the ceiling soaring above us, at one end a mezzanine floor on which the orchestra was situated, the musicians in full highland uniform of a local regiment. They were playing some modern dance tune in that brassy, pompous way of the military trying to be trendy. The dancers moved around on a polished parquet floor the size of a football field.

"Come and dance." I looked up. It was one of the wives we had met earlier. She was flushed, her eyes bright, red hair falling down around her face to her waist. She pulled me up and tugged me onto the floor. I looked around. Vi was already up, being twirled around by a massive kilted highlander with a full red beard. It was some sort of Scottish reel, totally wild, with lots of yelling. My partner, whose name, I think, was Fiona, spun and swayed, her tartan dress flying. She was tall with a statuesque figure graceful and appealing.

When we came together in dance she molded her body into mine and I found my face buried in her hair and neck. She smelt of good soap and the scent of clean hair. As we came apart, momentarily her lips brushed my cheek and she looked into my eyes.

"Let's get off the floor."

I looked around, thinking, "This was not in the plans."

"There's a little bar in the dungeons," she said.

"Oh, okay," I said lamely.

She took my hand and led me down a dark hall, turned, put her arms around me and kissed me. It was quite wonderful and completely took my breath away. She laughed, and, holding my hand, led me into a stone chamber that had been turned into a cocktail bar.

The walls had been painted silver. The effect, with the great arched ceilings and stone flagged floors, together with hidden lighting, was dramatically sinister. We drank champagne cocktails, sat in a deep couch, and fairly slavered over each other. This situation was rapidly getting out of control. I had to do something, and quickly. I made some comment about the others. She made a disparaging remark. I insisted. She became abusive. I became alarmed. She started to make a scene. I decided to retreat. I finally made it to the table. Everyone was staring.

Vi was there with the others, "They tell me she's a man-eater," she smiled. "How did you get on?"

I told her of my adventures. Looking around I noticed everyone was smiling knowingly. Fortunately it was getting late, though some people were only just starting to party. It was now about two a.m. and our group, who were family types, decided to make a night, or rather, morning of it, so we got our stuff together and returned to the house of the children, gathered sleepy heads and headed home.

The rest of the trip passed too quickly, not giving us enough time to see everyone and then, as if it had all been a dream, we were back at 30,000 feet, only this time with a quiet and happy, sleepy and tranquil Vicky, all teething gone.

It was back to normalcy. My work progressed well. I received another contact from the company in Canada and was seriously contemplating a move. I felt I had done all I could to improve sales, and relations with all our customers were cordial, close, and mutually beneficial. I was ready for new challenges. The trip to England had made me want to be, if not in England, closer to the traditions and customs of that country. I thought perhaps Canada would be a good compromise. Though America had been kind to me, there were still enough differences to cause some unease.

I felt strongly about the monarchy for instance, and resented the antipathy sometimes voiced by friends. I missed the patina of age that was so common in English towns and architecture, the countryside, the manners and traditions of society, the pubs, the food, and the conversation. The trip home had been like a sip of good wine. I wanted more.

It was just at this time, undecided and confused, that Jamie, the gentlemanly Scot, reappeared in my life. He was teaching at a university in Augusta, Georgia, less than a couple of hours drive away. This was great. His wise head would put me straight. We had a few customers in the Atlanta area. I determined to visit them and stop and see him. It was odd to have someone to say good-bye to, odd and strangely touching. As I drove away I felt distinctly uneasy and depressed. Home is where the heart is, for sure.

His Lordship in Manhattan
Jamie Sandilands, Master of Torphichen

I reached the city later that evening and found Jamie's flat. He was his usual gruffly welcoming self, cantankerous, yet jolly at the same time. His little bed-sitter was scruffy and untidy with books everywhere, piled on chairs, tables, and even the floor. Papers fought for space with unwashed socks and half eaten pizzas still in their cartons.

"Sit down if you can find room," he said.

I moved some books off a beat-up looking divan and did just that. I was exhausted after the drive and just needed a drink, food, and bed.

Jamie disappeared for a moment and came back with a bottle of scotch and two rather grimy looking glasses, which he wiped perfunctorily with a hanky he produced from his shirt cuff in the manner of a conjurer revealing a rabbit. The glasses were filled generously and polished off, iceless.

We exchanged all the news. His was enormous. Dad, the 16th baron, had just died and as he was a widower, and Jamie the eldest, I was now talking to the 17th baron. He was leaving for Scotland at the end of the school year to take up the duties and responsibilities that the title bestowed. Amongst other things, this meant that he would have to live in a castle, part of which was built in the 12th century, near Edinburgh.

His wife had left him not too long ago, so he was on his own again. She was an American and no doubt rued having given him up, as otherwise she would have inherited the title, Jamie having received the mantle of Lord. No doubt there was money too, as well as substantial property. So all in all he was a good catch now.

We continued the evening at a neat little pubby café where all his academic chums were holding up the bar. We all drank far too much and listened to Jamie telling comical anecdotes.

He and his father had, apparently, not been on speaking terms, and one time Jamie had turned up at the castle unannounced and had been received icily with the words, "I hope you're not planning to stay too long. The servants will find it very inconvenient, as will I." This in a fully staffed six-storey castle of some hundreds of rooms and chambers.

Jamie's reply was a weak, "I'll try not to get in the way," and "I return to the States next week."

That night at dinner, served with all the sparseness of the Scottish aristocracy, candles burning in enormous sconces and candelabra, Dad at one end and Jamie at the other end of a table of gargantuan proportions, they dined on soup, fish, mutton, and suet pudding with treacle. The meal ended with the butler placing a bottle of a fine single malt scotch on a silver tray before his lordship and with somewhat less ceremony, a lesser, blended variety in front of James.

Four days later when he had completed the business he had to attend to, Jamie prepared to tell the maid to pack his bags, and, still not having had any communication with Dad, went down to the dining room for his last supper. Dad was, as usual, sitting at his end, but this time looked up from the paper he was reading and said, "Hear you're leaving tomorrow. Stay longer if you like," and went back to his reading. Jamie was so startled at this revelation that he could hardly eat the savoury. And it was not over yet. When the scotch came out, only the best one was served.

We staggered back to the flat where the party continued into the early hours with raging debates of an academic and obtuse nature. I left them, still arguing, at four in the morning. I had to get to a factory near Atlanta by ten, so needed some sleep. The day that followed was long and painful and I was glad when it ended.

I was staying that night with some friends, a couple I had known in Greensboro who had moved to Atlanta and opened a small ad agency. I had known the wife before she married and had had a brief but torrid affair with her. Now we were all good friends. This happy situation was about to change however, and the events of that night and the following weekend were going to affect my life in the most drastic fashion.

I arrived at Gerry's and Peggy's house at my preferred time for arriving anywhere, just in time for drinks.

Anyway, here I was getting welcomed, rather too warmly, by Peggy, who gave me an extremely provocative kiss. I was left gasping. The rest of the evening passed with more drink, supper, and trying to avoid the long, languorous looks Peggy kept giving me. She had, in addition, unbuttoned the top two fasteners of her blouse revealing more of her breasts than was decent. I knew that Gerry had a quick temper and was very possessive, and to make matters even more uneasy, possessed a large collection of hand guns which he proudly exhibited on the wall of his study, a nasty looking mixture of revolvers and automatic pistols, that he knew how to use.

Finally I made my excuses, did my toilet, and went to bed. I had only just rolled over, put out the light, and closed my eyes when the door opened with a squeak and flooded the room with light from the hall. Outlined against this illumination was Peggy's perfect Venus body in a nightie that left nothing to the imagination. I sat up startled and alarmed, "Shh," she mouthed and shut the door. 'God, this was too much.'

She got into bed and pulled the sheets up and turned to kiss me. Before I could decide the next course of events, temptation, mixed with my Catholic ethos, mixed with fear of violent reactions from Gerry, though he did seem very out of it when we parted earlier, perhaps now sleeping soundly, mixed with 'No, what am I thinking? I'm a newly married man, but then Peggy is rather luscious. Oh dear,' with a crash, the door was flung open. The light was switched on. It was Gerry, in full fury, face contorted with rage and malevolence. With a shriek, Peggy leapt out of the bed and flew past him screaming.

"It was his fault Gerry. I wouldn't never, never… ," her voice faded as she disappeared and I heard a door slam. I was in trouble.

"By God Teddy," he shouted, "You've abused my hospitality once too often. You've had it this time." He left me trying to dress in a hurry, but was back in a flash holding a very unpleasant looking pistol in one hand and cocking it with the other. His face was contorted with anger. The next few moments seemed like hours. As I struggled to put legs into trousers, time went by in slow motion.

I was trying to calm him down using as matter-of-fact a manner as I could, in view of the circumstances. I remember thinking, 'So this is where it's going to end, after going through the blitz and war at sea in the navy, three years in a most savage part of Africa, and other adventures in various exotic parts of the world, this is it, in some boring, obscure suburb, some non-descript street with ordinary houses filled with ordinary people.' Gerry meanwhile, was waving the gun around and yelling about loyalties and unfaithfulness.

I was now fully dressed and still protesting my innocence. I made my way to the front door and out into the cold night. Gerry followed me threateningly. I was now in the car, turning on the ignition and pretending that nothing was happening, I reversed out to the street, into first gear and roared away. It was then that I realized, that although I had had the presence of mind to even put my tie on, I had forgotten to put shoes and socks on. I didn't think I would go back for them somehow.

It was months later that George Fortescue, who had been their best man, told me that they played that whole scene as a game, the seduction and irate discovery *in delecto*, was the way they got their jollies. Very amusing, I don't think.

⁂ ⁂ ⁂ ⁂

The next day I had appointments including one for lunch at a snazzy downtown restaurant. Just as I was calling for the bill at the end of the meal, some sort of commotion was taking place outside in the street. We went out to find pandemonium everywhere. A black woman was on her knees in front of me in a position and attitude of supplication. People all around were standing in groups with looks of disbelief and grief on their faces. Police cars, sirens moaning, careened past. I went towards a cluster of people surrounding a man with a ghetto blaster on his shoulder. They were all listening intently to an announcer.

I listened, only half understanding the message. A Texas school book depository, a motor cavalcade, shots fired, Dallas, Oswald. "What? What was that? Kennedy, the beloved President of the United States. What? No. There must be some awful mistake. Perhaps... . Shot? Is dead? Oh, this is awful. This is the stuff of nightmares. This can't be."

Tear-streaked faces looked at me blankly. They looked so lost, so bewildered, so hopeless. Why would anyone cut off so brutally, someone the whole world respected and loved and who was seen as the example to follow into a new fresh world of hope, responsibility, and peace. I returned to my parked car and began my long drive back to Greensboro to be with my family, chastened, thoughtful, and contrite.

* * * *

There were messages waiting for me to call the American parent company of the firm in Canada that wanted to hire me. Apparently this corporate giant, out of Louisville Kentucky, desired to interview me before the Canadians were allowed to take me on. I called them at their Louisville headquarters and was asked to report, for an interview at their New York offices. Henceforth, I made the necessary arrangements and flew there the following week. I always stayed at the Vanderbilt Hotel in New York, partly through sentimental reasons, it being where Laura and I had met for a drink so long ago, and partly because it was close to the shopping district where many of the department and furniture stores were that I had to visit for research.

The offices were at the other end of 5th Avenue, so I caught a cab, and, as always when in New York, sat back and gazed entranced at the canyons of concrete and steel and glass that towered up all around, only half listening to the cabby who was going on about the difficulties of driving a cab in the city. We pulled up at an imposing building.

"Here you are buddy." I looked at the meter and paid the bill with much too large a tip. For some reason that I have never been able to fathom, I tend to be over the top a bit when it comes to largesse. Perhaps the desire to please, perhaps the thought that there but for the grace of god…, maybe a mixture of both with a dash of my strong dislike of meanness. Whatever it was, it exacted a response of effusive gratitude from the chauffeur, and gave me a warm lift.

I sprinted up the steps leading to a revolving door through which was passing a grey-suited horde of hopeful looking young men like myself. I found, upon consulting a directory, that the company was on the top ten storeys. The elevator whisked us up to the floor that housed the executive offices, stopped, and I got out.

It was all hustle. Well-groomed men hurried by with sheaves of important-looking papers in hand. Pretty girls similarly burdened, walked quickly past. They all had one thing in common. Their look was of absolute confidence and excessive importance.

I straightened my back, pulled my head up, adjusted the tie, and approached the front desk with more aplomb than I actually felt.

"Can I help you?" Looking up, the receptionist, perfect in every detail, smiled. A faultless example of the cosmetic side of dentistry was revealed. Mouth a slash of crimson, eyes bright, alert, mascaraed with care, nose *retrousse* and dilated.

"Er, I have an apartment, I mean an appointment, er, with Miss Thompson, your head colour stylist."

"Oh yes, certainly sir." She checked a list on the desk. "That's at ten." It was now coming up to that time. "Would you care to sit down? Can we bring you anything, coffee, tea, coke?"

"No thanks. Nothing for me, but thanks."

I settled back in a leather sofa that looked like it had just come out of the museum of modern art. It was black with shiny steel, elongated and stylish, Scandinavian in its simplicity.

"Mr. Payne?" My design peregrinations were interrupted. I looked up. A short, elegant, handsome woman of indeterminate age stood before me, a friendly smile on her face. We shook hands. "My office is on the next floor in the design department."

She led the way, asking politely about my flight, all the usual pleasantries. "Here we are." She opened a door that led into an enormous high-ceilinged room. It was obviously in the corner of the building as it had two floor-to-ceiling windows at right angles to each other. Now I knew that meant someone of importance occupied this office.

The furnishings were incredible: all very contemporary and clean-lined but with the odd antique spotted here and there. Only two pieces of art on the walls, but what pieces, one an early Picasso drawing, the other an original Matisse painting. They must have been worth a fortune. She seemed pleased when I complimented her on them. The view outside was, however, the main attraction. A magnificent panorama of the city lay below. We were on, I surmised, about the thirtieth floor, so one could see for miles. A haze in the distance only served to accentuate the visible skyscrapers nearby. How anyone could concentrate and work in this eyrie in the sky was beyond me.

I perched on a Herman Miller chair of impeccable lineage, slightly uncomfortable with all these surroundings. "Well Mr. Payne, what can we do to help you?" I blurted out the facts that had led me to be sitting in her office. She looked at me with a puzzled expression.

"Excuse me for a moment." She spoke into a

phone and told someone at the other end to come to her office. While we waited for this person to arrive, we talked in generalities, though I got the feeling that she really had no idea who I was and what I was doing in her office. This vague but uneasy sense was confirmed by the arrival of the summoned one.

He turned out to be VP in charge of personnel, and who, after introductions, and the consulting of some filed papers in his hand, said "Louisville's dropped the ball again. There is no advice of your purpose in being here, just that you were to be expected and that more information would follow. It hasn't, so perhaps you would fill us in."

Oh boy, this was awkward. I explained the history of my relationship with the company so far, which took all of half an hour.

They looked at each other and she said, "Well I'm terribly sorry you've come all this way for nothing, but I'm afraid there is nothing we can do to advance the process of hiring you without more consultations with Louisville."

The way she said it indicated to my bruised ego that she couldn't much care either. She stood, shook hands limply, and said to the other person "Joe, take Mr. Payne down, would you?" The descent to the lobby seemed to take forever, but when I found myself on the street outside with the revolving doors thumping behind me, I felt as though it had only been seconds since I had entered earlier.

Feeling thoroughly let down, I called a cab and

went back to the hotel. I hurriedly packed my bag, checked out of the room, and took a taxi to the airport. Luckily there was a flight that was about to take off. I was ticketed and by dint of some hard sprinting made it to the plane as they were about to close the doors.

* * * *

Back home all was well on the domestic front, but in turmoil at work. There was a lot to catch up on and so I had to really work hard and concentrate on sorting things out. A good part of our work was to service existing accounts and my absence had been noticed adversely by some of our bigger customers. These giants bought enormous amounts of product from us amounting to hundreds of thousands of dollars, so a certain amount of ingratiation had to be undertaken.

Some weeks later I finally received an apologetic letter from the firm in Louisville explaining the mix-up in New York and confirming that though there was nothing with their company that would interest me, the Canadian subsidiary wanted me, so I was back to where I had been before all the mix-up had occurred.

The company in Canada contacted me very soon after getting back. It was located in a city called London,

Ontario, which seemed like a good omen, and the timing was for me to start work in the following autumn. As it was now coming up to Christmas, I had lots of time to finish things up here. There was a lot to do. Business was brisk. We had added considerable new customers to supply and service. My hands would be full.

✳ ✳ ✳ ✳

The winter of the Carolinas went by with the usual unpleasant combination of freezing rain, sleet, and wet snow that came down in the early morning and was gone by noon, and cold rain that drained the spirits and made the torturous drive down the mountains, where the Virginian factories were located, to the plains where I lived, more unnerving than usual. It was with much gratitude that I would arrive home to a welcoming Vianne and happy Vicky, martini put into hand, a roaring fire lit, and the sound and smell of cooking from the kitchen. Those were good days indeed.

✳ ✳ ✳ ✳

The spring came early and was, as always, the best part of the year in that latitude. The Dogwood blossoms in full flower, the fields green, peppered with yellow, the air fresh and mild.

The April furniture market was to open in a few weeks and we were busy preparing all the new designs for all our customers. This was the busiest time of the furniture year. The shows were held twice a year, now and in the fall, and were attended by buyers from all over the country, and indeed from many parts of the world. This was the moment we were on stage. As soon as the shows were over, we settled into our routine of domestic bliss.

Life was quite idyllic: work hard all day, home by seven, a martini on the rocks waiting, a kiss from Vi, and Vicky on my lap playing with my tie. Watching the news on TV though, was enough to spoil this picture of contented married life. The picture we watched with horror showed the KKK louts shooting some freedom fighters from the north. It didn't help to know that this was happening only a few streets from where we were sitting.

It was the early sixties when the strife between black and white in the area was at its peak. There were sit-ins and violent encounters daily. I had two experiences, one that shocked and nauseated me, and the other that gave me back my faith in some human conduct.

The first instance occurred when we were playing cricket. I should explain that I had formed a team from exchange students that were attending some of the local colleges. There were three Trinidadians, a Jamaican who was our demon bowler, a couple of New Zealanders, a professor from India, some Brits who lived locally and the balance made up of American chums who were fascinated by the game and who learnt quickly as they were already fine athletes and could play baseball, which has some vague similarities to cricket.

It was, I think, only the second or third game we played. It was against the team fielded by the University of North Carolina, who had a similarly composed side to ours, inasmuch as it was made up from students from the British Commonwealth and a few Americans. The game took place in Greensboro at our rough-and-ready field.

Anyone who knows anything at all about the game knows that the part where the ball is in play between the bowler and batter should be smooth closely cut grass or matting as the ball has to bounce before arriving at the batsman's end. We had no such luxury, our pitch being coarse grass with many imperfections. Therefore the ball behaved in a most unruly and sometimes unexpectedly violent manner. On the occasion in question it ricocheted from the ground, traveling at speed, and hit the unfortunate batsman in the nose, breaking it. The ball, I might add, is made of leather, is red in colour, and is very hard.

The game was held up as we applied cold compresses to the bleeding face of Mahash Jaipur, for it was the doctor of physics from India who was the victim. When we saw the damage that had been done, we rushed the poor fellow to the local hospital's emergency room, where we were dumfounded to hear that he could not be treated there as he was coloured, and had to go to the facility for Negroes.

After an extremely acrimonious altercation we resigned ourselves to the humiliation we had been subjected to, and took poor Mahash to the other hospital where he was looked after. This was a negative example and one that went a long way in confirming my decision to move to Canada. But then there was the incident at a roadside trucker's restaurant on the way to Washington, where we were to play the British Embassy team.

We had stopped for a quick meal and were all tightly jammed around a table eating hamburgers and French fries, eight whites and our three West Indians, when we were approached by two men, big hairy-looking brutes they were.

"What are you niggers doing in here? Get the fuck outa here, now." I am not combative by nature, but being captain of the team, knew it was my responsibility to rise to the occasion. This I did, literally standing up and facing the enemy. What I was going to do next, I had no idea. At this juncture Jim Heaton, one of my American boys, a hard-bitten redneck type who had seen the light and was now the black lad's best buddy, came to the rescue. He vaulted the table, and in one of the most extraordinary feats of foot and fist work I had ever seen, made mincemeat of the two louts. Though everyone in the place took note of what was happening there was no interference. We paid our bills and left. So here was the obverse side of the coin. There were, and still are exceptions to every rule, and people can change.

We continued on to Washington where I opened the batting and was bowled out first ball by an elderly gentleman who wore a varicolored cap that I didn't recognize. On enquiry he said, "Palestine Police." I felt better. We got very drunk that night, reminiscing.

It was inevitable I suppose, that having chosen to take some chances in life, volunteering for the navy, going to Africa, coming to the States on a whim, that I would eventually run into trouble and I did on several occasions, but it seemed that there was always either someone to get me out of the situation, or that circumstances altered to allow myself extrication and retirement with honour intact.

At the end of the war, the ship I was serving on then, a cruiser of the Fiji class, HMS Jamaica, was ordered to the port of Surabaya in what used to be Java. We were to help the Dutch keep their colonies there and fierce and brutal fighting was going on all over the island.

One morning I was detailed as senior able seaman to take a shore patrol into the town. We consisted of a dozen young ratings, all boy seamen, fluffy around the chin, white and pink, just out of school. We were issued rifles, but no ammo. "You might hurt yourself," the master at arms said in a surly tone. I was given a thirty-eight Webley revolver, again sans ammo, webbing, equipment, and gaiters, and armlets that read "Naval Police." The last items to be handed us were, of all things, short navy cutlasses that looked more suitable for close quarter cut-and-thrust with Nelson, than being of utility in this, the atomic age.

We were put ashore from the motor cutter by the chief bosun's mate who admonished me to "Give 'em shit." It was stiflingly hot as I fell the lads in on the jetty, some very dubious looking locals looking on. I tried to sound martial and stern, but could only manage a sort of weak croaking sound that sounded like a very unwell frog.

"By the right, quick march." Off we went, our swords clanking uncomfortably on our hips.

When we arrived at the first corner that debouched onto the main street, pandemonium reigned. Trucks with Dutch marines looking exceedingly fierce and, apparently, very drunk, roared backwards and forwards on the street shooting in all directions. When a couple of rounds zinged over our heads and smacked into the wall behind, I decided that that was enough. I had no plans to die, now that the real war was over, so ordered the boys into an alley nearby where we could shelter. This was a bad mistake. Probably waiting to ambush somebody on the street behind was a mob of rebels with their backs to us. Consternation. They heard us and turned around.

Bugger those noisy swords, I thought. Without them, we could have skulked away. What now? The boys looked at me appealingly. At that moment a rock or brick, came sailing through the air from their general direction. It chose the wrong person to land on.

The one older boy in the group and a very rough individual from Newcastle, yelled in pain and then roared, "Fuck that," drew his cutlass and went hell-for-leather for the now startled looking enemy. They turned and fled, dropping all sorts of cutlery as they went. The rest of us followed pell-mell. We finally caught up with Geordie. He was standing, wiping his sword. The foe had vanished. I decided that it was time to go home. That night aboard, we were made much of and after some consumption of rum were exaggerating our feats to all and sundry.

* * * *

Once in Khartoum, not long after my arrival, there was a three-day riot caused by tribesmen loyal to the present arrangement, where, although the country was officially the Anglo-Egyptian Sudan, it was all really run by the British. The then-president of Egypt was visiting Khartoum to try to effect a change in this policy that would favour Egyptian influence. Nasser, though popular in his country, was universally despised in the Sudan and this was the emotion that was causing the locals to get belligerent. Oddly enough these were the very tribes that had fought so bravely against the British at the time of the Mahdi and the Khalifa Abdullahi in the late nineteenth century.

Anyway, here I was with the native clerks battening down the hatches, closing steel shutters on the windows, and generally looking as it must have done in the days of General Gordon. Ezzel din Effendi, my chief clerk, must have noticed the nervousness I was trying to hide, for he said in a mollifying tone, "It's alright Mr. Payne sir. We will look after you." So much for the act I was putting on.

Out on the streets, we were told later, general mayhem was taking place. Apparently the tribesmen had hidden swords, spears, and daggers in the folds of their clothing and were now attempting to get at Nasser and retinue, the police trying to keep them apart. Sadly, the chief of police, a wonderful, well-loved Irishman, was speared fatally while trying to expostulate with an over-excited warrior. His native chauffeur was also killed, trying to protect his beloved master. The ironic end of this tragedy was that the sheiks who ruled the errant tribe adored the police commissioner and bore his coffin in the funeral, followed by wailing followers. Nasser left hurriedly, knowing when he was not wanted, and he never returned.

I cannot leave the subject of individual bravery and

coolness under pressure without describing how my boss put down, single-handedly, a small but potentially nasty altercation within our office complex. The disturbance was to do with some complaint relating to the cleaning staff. They had violently entered the building we occupied and were milling about in the central hall, a great looming, cool, green-tiled area, which housed an ancient horizontal engine. I always felt as though I were inside some sort of marine cave whenever passing through.

They were shouting, waving sticks and generally behaving in a menacing and unseemly way. I was peering through the door, ready to slam and lock at the first sign of trouble, when down the stairway came himself, member-of-the-most-excellent-order-of-the-British-Empire, military-class, wearing, as always, white shirt, long grey trousers, and old Westminster school tie, pale, icy blue eyes at the ready. He strode confidently up to the mob and threaded his way through to where he knew the ringleader was standing. Taking hold of the individual by the elbow he said, "Now, now Abdul, we can't have this, come and see me in the morning and we'll talk," all the time gently leading him out to the street beyond the door.

The rest followed meekly. As he walked back to the stairs, he saw me peeping out. He clapped his hands together and said, "Well well Payne, back to work." I thought, this was and is, the way the Empire was run, bluff and the confidence created by a public school education.

* * * *

I had to go to Manhattan again to make a survey of what was selling in that area as regards styles and colours of case goods furniture. I would go to all the big stores: Macy's and Gimbel's, as well as to several smaller shops and decorator boutiques, interview the buyers, and then write and mail out a report to all our customers.

I called Jamie as soon as I got there and we arranged to meet. It was a freezing cold night and by the time I got to the bar where we were to meet I was really ready for something to drink that would relax my seized-up bones. Jamie was leaning against the bar holding forth to an admiring group. It was extraordinary how this aristocratic Brit could hold the attention of a totally blue-collar collection of people. The bar was in a working class neighbourhood with a reputation that was not exactly savoury. They were captivated by his stories and by the way he told them. They adored him.

"Teddy." He introduced me around. A drink was shoved in my hand, bourbon and water. I lit up and relaxed. This was great. "I say, Teddy, I hope you don't mind, I have to go and see an aunt of mine. She's expecting me for dinner and said to bring you. Hope you don't mind?" I did a bit. I was looking forward to a bar crawl. To stay here would have been alright, but I said I wouldn't mind, so off we went to find a cab.

The wind was howling down the canyon. We were standing amid bits of paper that went flying by. The pavement under my feet rang as I walked. The world seemed suddenly brittle and hard. I noticed Jamie had no overcoat and had stuffed the day's paper under his shirt and underwear. Bits of rumpled newspaper stuck out of unbuttoned crevices. He looked like a street bum looking for a handout.

A taxi finally came to a stop nearby and we got in. I saw the driver looking at Jamie in a very doubtful way, but after some directions that I couldn't hear we were off, driving in that peculiar way that New York cabbies do, fast, with little body movement, soaring from bump to bump, talking without stop, the chewing gum contorting their face and making their dissertation on the city and its faults totally incomprehensible.

I was not a little surprised when we stopped at the front entrance of a very classy block of flats on Park Avenue. Then I remembered Jamie telling me once about the American side of his family. His mama came from old New England stock, Oyster Bay, I believe, and had lots of money. I paid off the driver, who was now looking at us with new respect, and we went through the door opened by a commissionaire, who knew Jamie.

"Good evening sir."

"Evening Roberts," said Jamie, still sprouting newsprint from every aperture. I was mortified. We entered a small lift. Jamie pushed a floor button, we climbed noiselessly and with great speed, stopped, and the doors opened to reveal a hall with a living room beyond. It seemed odd to get off an elevator and go directly in to the apartment without a corridor and front door in between.

A middle-aged, but still beautiful woman came up smiling, "Jamie, how lovely to see you," this while Jamie was tugging at bits of paper still protruding.

"Yes, er, hello. Margo, this is Teddy Payne."

"How do you do Mr. Payne," giving me a captivating smile and a dry handshake.

"Very well, thank you Mrs. er…" Jamie had neglected to give me her name.

"Oh call me Margo," she said. "Jamie, when are you going to buy some new underwear? You are tiresome. For goodness sake give me all that rubbish." She pulled at the newspaper.

"No, no I've not finished reading it yet," answered Jamie plaintively.

"Oh, I give up," she said in exasperation. "Come in and have a drink. Everyone is dying to see you and meet your friend."

We followed her into a large sunken living room with about half a dozen people standing around with drinks in their hands. Margo, who was the aunt, and whose flat this was, made the introductions: her husband, a distinguished silver-haired gentleman; an exceedingly glamorous woman dressed and bejeweled who held out a languid hand; her husband, equally caparisoned; a younger man who, I sensed was gay, his handshake was more of a squeeze and his eyes sent a signal that I could not mistake, he was the son of the two I had just met; and lastly, a pretty teenager dressed in the American private school costume of white blouse and dangerously attenuated tartan skirt.

We all sat down and a maid passed around with cocktails on a tray. "Would you like martinis or Manhattans?" Margo asked. "We've got both. Or would you like something else? scotch, beer, or perhaps you don't drink."

"That's a laugh," said Jamie. I picked a glass off the tray trying to think of something witty to say in response, but was put off by the sight of the school girl who was sitting opposite me very slowly crossing her legs and looking intensely and meaningfully into my eyes.

I started to check around my surroundings. The room was quite stupendously furnished in an eclectic manner, an understated but elegant combination of antique pieces sitting happily cheek-by-jowl with some fabulous Miller modern chairs and tables. From the distance the paintings and drawings on the wall looked impressive. I hoped to get a better look later.

General conversation commenced, accompanied by much drinking and laughter. Although not one of the family, I was included as if they had known me all their lives. Americans of the old money class are really quite superior. Not only are they interesting and have good manners, they are interested in many other things as well, which, I believe is one up on the British upper classes who tend to have limited interests, and those of a horsy bent as a rule.

We sat down to a lavishly laid table: napery, glassware, cutlery and plates all of the highest quality and design. The meal was plain but delicious, the wine, memorable. The only fly in the ointment was the girl who had made a beeline for the chair next to me and spent much of the time stroking my upper thigh and knee and being flirtatious in the extreme. I tried to be aloof in a polite way. This seemed only to inflame her further.

She suddenly said to no one in particular, "Let's do the town. I've only got a day left before I go back to school and I've not really had any fun." Everyone looked doubtful. "You'd like to go out wouldn't you Teddy?" She looked at me appealingly.

"Oh, er, sure," says I.

"Come on everybody, let's go to the Village." She continued, "And perhaps later we can go dancing at Birdland." Taxis were sent for and we all trooped down to the lobby. Thankfully Jamie didn't replace the paper.

Thus began one of the wildest evenings of my life. First we went to the Village, to a well-known pub called the White Horse Tavern, famous at the time for being the bar where Dylan Thomas allegedly drank himself into a stupor every night and eventually into an early grave. The place was packed with the Beat Generation, the predecessors of the flower children, the hippies. There was sawdust on the floor, tobacco smoke filled the air, the noise was incredible, a steady hum of conversation punctuated with bursts of laughter, the clatter of glass and the tinkle of a piano being played in a dissonant manner somewhere in the back.

We found a table and ordered several large jugs of beer. We had attracted some attention when we first came in, the locals seeing us as squares from uptown slumming, but after a while they ignored us. At one point a young man rode in on a unicycle, pedaled up to the bar and ordered a drink. This was all too hilarious for words. By now the young girl, whose name was Lisa, was really getting amorous and, I have to admit, so was I.

I tried to make conversation in an effort to slow down any progression in that department, and made sure the others were well into the conversation. It seemed to help a little. She told me that she was going to Vassar, one of the better Eastern schools, and that she would be graduating next year. That made me feel better, as that would make her at least seventeen. "Thanks for small mercies," I thought.

It was now well past midnight. Everybody wanted to go to Birdland to dance. Bills were paid and out into the freezing night we went, Lisa clutching my arm.

Jamie, in front, turned and almost slipped on the now icy pavement, his glasses glittered, his cheeks rosy, nose to match. He squeaked in his falsetto voice, "Jesus Christ." He looked like Father Christmas out on the town. Thankfully we didn't have to wait for a cab. By now we were tight enough to try to squeeze into one taxi by dint of sitting on laps, and, unusually for NY, two were allowed to sit in front with the driver. We sang and laughed all the way to the ballroom.

Birdland was then a very popular dance hall of monumental proportions. It was always packed and always had name bands. This was the time of Jazz that was called progressive: Stan Kenton and Miles Davis were names of the day. The style was dissonant, noisy and brassy. It was the sound of the fifties and the Beat Generation. We literally danced the night away.

Finally we'd all had enough, though Jamie still wanted to take us to an after-hours club that he had just joined. Only Lisa and I would go, and I was definitely fading, so we all made fond farewells vowing to meet again. We never did. Lisa, Jamie, and I set off without the others. This was my first mistake.

The club was a disappointment. Gloomy and Germanic. Why Jamie ever joined was beyond me. For some reason he enjoyed the company of rather brutish Teutons, not my favourite type. As soon as we got in the place we were inundated with the Hun, who took especial interest in Lisa, a fact to which I took exception. The drink had by now made me feel cross and belligerent and I rather foolishly decided to fight WWII again.

All these individuals were of an age that would have put them at the other end of a weapon to me back in the late forties. They all protested that they had fought on the eastern front against the Russians, and I remarked that if they were all in Russia who the hell was shooting at me? They laughed, but there was not much humour in it.

Latterly it began to get ugly and I had to beat a strategic retreat accompanied by the girl who by now was looking a bit pale. Jamie defiantly stayed. She and I struggled up the stairs to the cold outside. The club was in a deserted side street and I had no idea where I was.

We found our way to a main street that turned out to be 3rd Avenue on the Lower East Side, a not very salubrious neighbourhood. By sheer chance, an off-duty cab with all lights doused, decided to stop. I directed him to the apartment building on the Upper East Side where Lisa lived and turned to hopefully receive her approbation in the form of some indication of affection, to be greeted by a long and decidedly unappealing snore.

When we got to the flats, the commissionaire had to be roused to let her in. He practically had to carry her, giving me a look of intense disapproval. I fell back in the back seat of the cab and gave the driver Jamie's address in Brooklyn. He very smartly came to a screeching stop. "Can't take you there."

"Why not?" says I.

"Too dangerous at this time of night." It was actually two or three in the morning. "And I won't be able to get a fare back. You'll have to get out." He clicked the meter up, turned and looked at me. "You'll have to get the subway. Take the IRT to the bla, bla, bla, then take the A train to yatterty, yatterty, yatterty, etc., etc.," totally incomprehensible.

I offered to give him a really handsome tip if he would at least take me to the nearest subway station. He agreed. We roared off and came to a precipitate halt around the next corner. I handed him the fare and tip with what I hoped was a look of intense hatred. Down the steps I went, now feeling quite sober and in control. I went to the ticket booth and explained my plight. Ignorant of what the form was, where I was, and how to get to where I wanted to go. The official was kind and helpful in a slightly condescending way, but I was past caring.

I found my way to the platform of departure and was immediately struck by the atmosphere of dilapidation and dirtiness. The infrastructure had seen better days and cleanliness did not seem to be a concern. The smell of unwashed bodies and urine pervaded, rubbish lay all around, discarded newspapers and other detritus scattered about, the track being particularly noisome.

The clientele matched the surroundings, appearing to be figures of some criminal intent. After a quick look around, I decided the platform should have my attention. I had learned long ago to avoid eye contact in moments of possible confrontation, so stood gazing fixedly at my feet.

There was a sudden onrush of sucking air and with a thunderous clattering roar, the train exploded into the station flashing blue electrical sparks. Illuminated passengers in the coaches. It was an entrance that brought with it a feeling of some relief, bringing light, life, and normalcy to the gloom of the platform.

The doors opened and the world became real and ordinary again. The figures of suspicion became commuters anxious to reach their homes in Queens, White Plains, and New Jersey. I found a seat, lit a cigarette and relaxed. The train went directly to my destination, Atlantic Avenue, which was reached after a few moments of smelly, noisy discomfort. It was with some relief that I reached the open air, cold as it was but infinitely preferable to the fog I had just left.

It was with even more satisfaction that I arrived at Jamie's apartment block. Oh for my bed, nice and cozy. Perhaps a cup of cocoa. Yes, that would be nice. Here's the door. I knocked. No answer, tried the handle, locked. Banged again, silence. Curses. He was still out on the town.

I settled down on the floor, shoes as pillow, overcoat my blanket. I slept. Needless to say the night was extremely uncomfortable and I was relieved when Jamie finally turned up and released me from my bed of pain.

We spent most of the day, a Sunday, sleeping until noon, at which time we ate bacon sandwiches and drank beer. More sleep followed, replenishing our vital juices and giving us the strength to face the oncoming evening and its promise of more dissipation.

Jamie had promised to take me to his favourite New York bar, a place called the Tokay. It was somewhere down on the southwestern end of Manhattan, not what one would describe as a choice location, but Jamie assured me that it was reasonably safe and that lots of characters hung out there. We set out in a taxi, driving through a damp foggy night, the streets wet, reflecting the lights of the shop windows. As we passed an especially garishly lit liquor store, Jamie remarked, "Now that's a cheerful sight."

We arrived after some moments of trepidation caused by the driver's attempts at short-cutting down narrow alleys and crossing main streets as we traveled against the grain of the city and its north-south traffic flow. As Jamie was paying the driver, I looked about me. The scene was like something from a Bogart movie I know. It was "Across the Pacific," the rotund and sinister Sydney Greenstreet and that sexy Canadian, Mary Astor, came to mind.

We were close to the docks and I could see ships funnels and masts quite near. In the foreground were dockside buildings and warehouses with cranes and gantries silhouetted against the glare of yellow high-powered lamps, the whole picture made more dramatic by the mist that swirled around fitfully.

As the cab drove away, the silence was intense, broken only by the sound of someone walking quickly in another street. The footsteps rang loudly on the pavement, faded and disappeared. It wasn't cold, but I shivered momentarily and turned to follow Jamie into the Tokay bar. The door opened and light and cheerful loud chatter and laughter spilled out onto the street.

It seemed that everyone knew Jamie. He was embraced and greeted by one and all. I was continually impressed by Jamie's ability to attract people of all types and all classes. Here he was, the son of a Lord being made much of by dockyard stevedores, factory hands, and the like, most of them looking as though they didn't have much to lose. In any event, it was marvelous. We had a wonderful evening.

The bar was owned by an ex-cavalry officer from Budapest, hence the name of the place, Tokay, who had served in the Africa Corps with Rommel, and prior to that, in the French Foreign Legion, so lots of interesting conversation ensued. Other notables were movie stunt men, labour union types, tough-talking and bruised-looking but gentle as lambs with Jamie and me, seamen scarred and alert, some cops in plain clothes. Very much at home, we drank and told jokes, drank and laughed until our tears ran, vowed eternal friendships and made promises to meet again.

The latter part of the evening faded into obscurity, but I do remember being helped into a car in an atmosphere of much *bonhomie* by the policemen and realizing that we were getting a lift at the expense of the citizens of Manhattan. We wailed across town to Brooklyn, skidding blissfully round corners and screaming through red lights at top speed. After that, the recollections blur, though I do remember thinking, 'God, this is life imitating art for sure.' I could almost hear the tune from "Laura" with the ravishing Gene Tierney and the dour, young Dana Andrews.

I worked the stores for the last few days in New York, cruising Bloomingdale's, Lord & Taylor's, some of the specialty furniture shops and decorators, interviewed buyers and designers and wound up the week at Gimbel's and Macy's.

Next day, in the evening, loaded with notes and photographs, I got on the Silver Star Express at Penn station for the train ride to the Carolinas. This trip was an event in itself and is worth describing.

The moment one made the easy step from platform

to train coach floor, one was in Dixie. "Yes sir. This way sir. Welcome aboard sir." This accompanied by much bowing and saluting, the bags taken gently from the hands, the teeth white as pearls, the gums pink as bubble gum, enormous grins splitting the great black wonderful face. One was embraced by this strong comforting presence.

Shepherded and guided along the narrow corridor that hummed and glistened and smelt of coffee and cleanliness, a door opened, revealing a small space with upholstered bench on one side, and a door to the bathroom opposite. A large picture window looking out on the dark and cold platform completed the picture. It all looked so cozy and warm and was to be my home for the next ten hours or so.

The porter explained various functions of switches and levers that activated climate controls, lighting and such, and told me about dinner and where it could be eaten and when, where the bar car was, and when he would be making my bed up, for it was now about seven o'clock.

Left alone, I settled down and looked around me. This was alright. It's a lovely feeling, I think, to start out on a long journey on a train knowing that you can relax. No one can get to you. One is virtually cut off from the rest of the world. You will be looked after and later be swung to sleep in the luxury of a comfy bed while the travel continues.

As I cogitated smugly, there was a hoot from the

locomotive and with a jerk the train moved away, gliding almost noiselessly between the two platforms. Figures and objects like barrows and other impedimenta of the station went past. The window lights blurred and flashed advertisements for Broadway shows that briefly attracted attention and were gone before conscious recognition had taken place. Then, swoosh… stygian darkness. My face lit up, hand on chin, cigarette burning.

I looked at myself curiously. Teddy, Ted, Tony. I had tried calling myself that once, thinking it sounded sexier, or at least less childish. It didn't help with the fairer sex however, and I reverted to Teddy.

Then I thought of all the places I had been to: England, Egypt, and Palestine as a child, the rolling main during the war at sea, Africa, India, Burma, Java, Malaya, Ceylon, America, Canada, and the Persian Gulf, and many of the islands of those oceans, the Seychelles, Mauritius, Zanzibar and Sumatra. Some at peace, some with the noise of battle. God I had been so lucky. I had been spared injury or worse. I had not had to deal with desperate suffering or scenes of gore and tragedy. The ship had been lucky and happy, the camaraderie, splendid and authentic.

My mind really started to wander then, as I remembered with sadness my mates, especially the two old queens who ran the canteen where we bought cigs and sweets and books. When I say old, they were in their early twenties I suppose; we were in our mid-teens. Now we had all heard the jokes about the queers as they were then called, and not to bend over in the showers and that sort of thing, so we were always wary of what might be perceived as unusual attention from older hands, particularly of these strange creatures. One must remember also that homosexuality was a forbidden practice then and subject to strict and brutal punishment. Nonetheless it did exist and one had to be careful.

However, we received nothing but kind motherly attention from them, especially in times of crisis, which was frequent in the North Atlantic. They would comfort the frightened and sometimes tearful boys in the same way as their mums. As well, in times of real stress and danger, they were as brave as women are when protecting their young. I had, and still do have, the greatest respect for much of their kind.

I remember the kindly but vague officer who told me I would not have to climb masts as a radar rating, as I feared heights, but then when the *moment critique* occurred in mid-Atlantic, in a storm at night, sitting in the mess playing cards, with a great commotion of water splashing and wind sound, the hatch above our heads opened and an oil-skinned figure came clattering down the ladder. It was the chief bosun's mate. He stood there, red-faced and staring-of-eye, water dripping off the peak of his cap.

" 'Oo's duty hand?" There was a second or two of silence. He glared around.

"I, er, suppose, er, I am chief," I said meekly.

"Right, get your kit together and report to me up top. We've got to fix the 281 aerial on the foremast."

My heart sank. This was right at the top. We had unusually high masts on this ship, some two hundred feet high. The aerial was reached by a narrow ladder attached to the slender steel mast. Halfway up was the yardarm and lookout position, which had to be negotiated by using a rope ladder that was secured in an intermittent fashion. I swallowed hard and said, "But chief, they told me at barracks that I didn't have to climb masts." Spared, I thought.

He looked at me unbelievably. Chief bosun's mates held enormous authority and possessed great prestige. The wags would say they were like Jesus Christ promoted a couple of times.

"Get up top with your gear before I boot you up the arse." He turned and clumped up the ladder and disappeared into the rain and darkness above.

I climbed miserably after him pulling on my oilskin and lifebelt. Reaching the upper deck, I saw him with another sailor preparing to hoist a bag of tools to a figure already halfway up the mast.

The wind howled and the ship rolled and plunged in the sea that was getting rougher by the minute. How was I going to get through this nightmare? The chief looked round and motioned me to start climbing. I began to mount one rung at a time. I thought, perhaps if I really try, if I keep my eyes shut, I might make it. Don't look down. The remonstrances back at training camp came back to me. It seemed easy then, fifty feet above ground on an assault course. The ground wasn't moving like this ship was.

I looked up. The tip of the mast, which I could just see lit by the glare from the funnel sparks, was moving in a great circle against the dark ragged clouds. I couldn't resist, I glanced downwards, and almost fainted. I was much higher than I had thought and more frightened than ever. I froze, hugging the mast and prayed.

"Awl right son, let's have you." It was the chief. He had followed me up and was now balancing somehow on a projection of some kind, his face level with mine. He grasped me around the waist and gently but firmly loosened my hands from their death grip. He held me in his massive arms and we fumbled and slid down to the upper deck.

I stood shaking with fear and cold, wet through and ashamed. The others stared at me in my humiliation. "Awl right my lad, you get aft to the galley and get some hot kye." This was the thick hot creamy sweet cocoa that was always available. "Then get in your hammock. You're excused duty. We'll say no more about it." God I was lucky.

My dreaming was interrupted suddenly by a discreet tap at the door. It was the porter. "Dinner is now being served in the dining car, sir. I'll make up the bed while you're gone, if that's alright." I said that that would be fine.

He shut the door, and I turned to the little bathroom. It was tiny. There was barely room to stand up, let alone do the more complicated tasks that are involved when attending to human functions of hygiene. I managed to complete what we used to call a French wash.

How awful we Brits are sometimes when talking about other nationalities. I remembered what my father used to call Egyptian PT. This referred to sleeping. No wonder they hated us in the Middle East. But it seemed funny at the time. We would make fun of the Welsh too, for some reason. Of course all the jokes were usually of a scatological nature whatever nationality was the butt.

I noticed most humour in America tended to be based on matters of a sexual nature, often at the expense of women, and frequently unkind in their content. I sometimes wondered at the covert and occasionally overt, negative attitudes to the female sex in the States. I could never fathom the reasons or their basis, but it was there.

But back to the task in hand, a bit of deodorant to the armpits, slick the hair down with some water and a brisk brush, a flick of the hanky to the shoes for the shine, straighten the tie, and off to the bar car for a quick one before dinner.

I swayed and stumbled my way two cars to the Pullman, pushing those buttons that open connecting doors that slid with a swoosh letting in icy air momentarily, the floor between them seemingly about to detach themselves from each other and looking alarmingly impermanent. Clatter, crash. A second of surreal metallic activity and then velvet, the sound of a tinkling piano playing Gershwin, a faint scent of perfume and bourbon and tobacco, a low hum of genteel conversation, a steward, his blackness exaggerated by the starched white uniform he wore.

"Good evening sir. This way. We're a bit full tonight. Would you mind sharing a table?" He motioned me to a small round table with two seats, one occupied by an extremely attractive woman.

"No not at all," I said. She looked up and smiled. "D'you mind?" says I.

"Not in the least." she replied. I sat down and looked up at the waiter who had arrived from nowhere.

"A double martini please. Very dry."

"Yes sir, comin' right up."

I looked at her. She was taking a cigarette from a pack of Winstons. "Would you like one?"

"Thank you." I took one from her and pulled out some matches, striking one. Waiting for the flame to flare and subside, I held it to the cigarette in her mouth. She leaned forward, the fingers of one hand touching my hand.

This was one of those magic moments that those who have never smoked have missed. The rituals and the paraphernalia of the cigarette were once such an important part of life. A cigarette was the first thing given, along with a cup of strong tea, to the survivor rescued from the rubble of a bombed house in the blitz. The Ronson lighters, the holder, such elegance, the engine-turned silver case one flicked open with such aplomb, the matchbooks from smart hotels. I'm glad I don't smoke anymore for obvious reasons, but I'm glad I experienced it once.

The light flickered and went out. It turned out that she was on her way to New Orleans, which is where the train ended its journey. She was a lawyer with a firm in New York and was going to defend an alleged murderer, who, it was said, had bumped off the wife for infidelity with his best friend. My martini arrived. I took a sip. It was perfect. We spent the next little while drinking more than we should, and eventually paid the bill and made our way, rather unsteadily, to the diner which was the next car.

There is something very glamorous about sitting in a diner at night, in a moving train, the lights flashing by, the bell clanging as roads are crossed, the swaying rattling coach. Usually the food is first class, and served with style. Silver service is the standard.

The meal over, we went back to the bar and had some brandy. If either of us had had any more ambitious plans for the rest of the evening, we were soon disabused of them by the fact that bed was needed for rest. Other activities being beyond our powers, we said goodnight with promises to meet again. These of course, never came to fruition.

❋ ❋ ❋ ❋

It was almost Christmas now, and Vianne and I were looking forward to our first together with our daughter. We bought the biggest tree we could find to suit the magnificent thirty-two foot ceilings. It was an imposing twenty footer. We dressed it in sparkling blue and silver iridescent balls and tiny brilliant white lights. With the other lights all out, an enormous fire in the grate, and the curtains drawn and carols in the background, it was a picture to savour. I thought, 'It can't get much better than this.'

❋ ❋ ❋ ❋

The winter passed and the lovely Carolina spring began. I had been asked by the Oak Association to do another lecture tour in England, this time a rather more ambitious affair. They had arranged three meetings. I was to be the principal speaker. Two were in London and one in High Wycombe, the furniture capital of the UK. Naturally I accepted.

One of the more appealing parts of the up-coming trip was that Jamie had invited us to stay with him at the castle he had inherited, so that as soon as I had finished the business part, I made arrangements to go up to Scotland by train. We went by sleeper again and left King's Cross in the late evening.

The journey was wonderful. We met some interesting people who owned a small island off the coast of Northumbria and knew Jamie's father. They described him as having been an eccentric. This of course I already knew.

We arrived at Edinburgh station next morning and got into a taxi. I asked the driver to take us to Calder House, the name of the castle. He twisted around to look at me and said in a rather stern manner, "That'll cost you a fiver."

"That's alright," I said.

"Well alright." He flicked off the meter and hunching up in a resigned fashion, drovc out of thc station yard, and glided down that most beautiful of all city thoroughfares, Princess Street.

We drove through the centre of the city gazing about at all the stunning architecture, the gardens, and the towering castle away over to our left. Leaving the grandeur behind, we passed through less imposing suburbs and light industrial areas, quite uninspiring, and in some cases positively ugly. We circled a roundabout, made a turn away from the detritus of the city and entered a more rural area that lasted for a short time.

When we arrived at the village of Mid Calder, it was really more of an extension of the city and seemed like a dormitory town for Edinburgh. Another turn and up a small hill to an enormous stone gateway complete with small gatehouse. The gate portico, I noticed, had frowning statues of eagles grasping a round rock.

Vicky at Calder House. Jamie's front gate.

"Is this it sir?" asked the driver.

"No, I think it's a bit further up the drive."

He turned and looked with surprise. "You mean up to the great house sir?"

"Yes, that's right."

He released the brake and through the gate we went. Obviously sentries were not on duty today. The drive wound around through deep high woods of pine and other coniferous trees, and was lined by round flat stones. There were hundreds of them. I found out later that these were the stones used over the centuries for curling on the lake that was on the property.

We swept around a long curve and the house came into view. Although it was called Calder House, it really was more a castle. High, at least six stories, with gothic cupolas at each corner, L-shaped in plan view, made of granite, with grand windows at the ground floor, apertures smaller as one looked higher, with, at the top, arrow slits. Jamie told me later that one wing was 12th century, the other a perfect copy built during the reign of Victoria.

"Look, there's Jamie." Vianne called out "Hi darling."

Jamie, standing in the doorway, grinning sheepishly, holding two martinis in each hand, God love him, said, "Hurry, dinner's served soon and I'm terrified of the servants." We laughed, not quite understanding the thrust of the comment. The driver helped unload and I gave him a handsome tip. He touched his cap and disappeared.

We walked into the hall, which was large and high and full of all the usual impedimenta of the great houses of Britain, heavily laden coat racks, overcoats, Mackintosh and Barbour, Burberry and Aquascutum, walking sticks, fishing rods and creels, caps and hats of every description, boots and shoes, and of course the inevitable green Wellies. The floor was flagstone, pink, and glistening with wax.

An elderly man appeared, dressed in rusty black with the horizontal striped waistcoat of the butler cum footman department. "Shall I take the luggage up m'lord?"

"Yes please do. You all have rooms at the top of the house. Sorry for the climb. The house is still mostly closed."

Pamela, Jamie's new wife, had to go to London today, so all the sorting out of furnishings and so forth had to stop. "She'll be back on Friday. Now, let's have a drink and go into dinner. You won't believe how strict the cook and the help are about mealtimes. They really run things here. I know it sounds odd, but the servant situation here is so bad. It's hard to run a house of this size without them. Impossible actually, and they know it. It's like having an invisible but powerful union. Oh dear. Here we are."

This room beggared description, first the sheer enormity of it all, lofty, soaring, cathedral-like ceilings disappearing into the gloom above. The floor, flagging of shiny polished stone, covered with Turkish and Persian rugs of such complex design and of such materials, silk probably, and wool, soft and luxurious to the foot, and no doubt, of an antiquity that matched the rest of the house. Along one wall, large paintings of men and women in the uniform and dress of the seventeenth and eighteenth centuries. A wood fire was blazing in a fireplace of gargantuan proportions.

The facing wall was lined with tall curtained French windows through which could be seen clipped hedges and topiary. In the distance, grey blue hills. The room was almost all taken up with a table of some magnificence, laid with silver and heavy white napery, candles flickering in sconces of silver. Glasses and condiment containers and various cruets completed the assemblage.

"Good afternoon Mrs. Macleod." Jamie spoke to a grey-haired uniformed woman who was bustling about with dishes and plates. She was closely attended by a younger girl who was helping.

"Good afternoon m'lord." They both bobbed. Soup was served, a marvelous broth rich and redolent with herbs and spices. This was followed by a cold plate of roast beef cut thinly, cold potatoes, and a salad. The dessert was fresh fruit and custard. All washed down by generous amounts of a brisk white wine.

The meal had hardly been finished when the help rushed in and cleared the table. "You see," said Jamie, "It wasn't like this in the old days. Would you like a rest? I expect you're both tired after the train journey."

"Yes, I wouldn't mind a nap."

"Nor would I," said Vianne.

"Alright, show my guests their rooms and the bathrooms etc." this to the retainer who had suddenly reappeared.

"Yes m'lord. Follow me please."

We started to climb the stone steps that wound slowly upstairs. Five landings we ascended until finally arriving at our floor. We followed the man, whose name we found was MacKintyre, down a long corridor, the walls of which were lined with prints of battles at sea of the Napoleonic period.

"Here we are madam and sir. This is your room and next door is the young lady's room." Vicky smiled with pleasure at being so addressed.

We looked around. Our room was light and cheerful. It looked like a nursery. It too had a fireplace in which a fire had recently been lit. The bed was large and comfy. There were bookcases everywhere full of those lovely red, blue, and green books of the twenties and thirties written by people like Baroness Orczy, Taffrail, and Edgar Wallace, about adventure, love, and murder-most-foul. Marvelous. I couldn't wait to get my hands on them. Vickie's room was smaller but just as cozy.

We next explored the bathroom. It was fantastic. A capacious tub of white enamel set in a sort of container of mahogany wood. Handsome taps controlled steaming hot water and towel racks were warm to the touch. Heavy Turkish towels were folded neatly on a chair. A bar of that lovely hard English soap smelling of oatmeal and lavender waited to be used.

We all had naps. I couldn't help noticing with a *frisson* of pleasure, the little tape of white cloth with red lettering sewed onto the blankets edging. "His lordship's blanket," it read. I went off into a deep sleep.

We went downstairs together at that time when tea is usually served, exploring as we descended. We found one great room that was lined with portraits that I supposed were of Jamie's ancestors. He later confirmed this and gave us a thumbnail sketch of most of them. Many of the paintings were by the great Scottish artist Raeburn. Most of the males were in uniforms of various periods. Some had fought with Robert the Bruce, some with the Pretender at Culloden, others in the forests of Canada and America against Indians, the French, and the rebels. The most recent works portrayed officers in the Napoleonic wars and there were even some in khaki from the Boer War.

Jamie explained that his family's connections went back to the time of Joan of Norway and the Scottish Order of the Knights Templar, who began their crusades to the Holy Land from the chapel that his family owned which was adjacent to the castle. Jamie was, I believe, the 17th Baron. An ancient family to be sure, with a house brimming with history.

We found him in the room in which he spent most of his time while they were fixing up the house. He had this enormous room, which was also obviously, the library, the walls lined with bookshelves, floor to ceiling, made into a sort of bed-sitter. There was a large fireplace blazing merrily away, comfy chairs and sofas, large tables on which were piled more books. A door led into a tiny butler's pantry in which one could prepare small meals. The mantelpiece held relics of past trips, photos of Pamela, as well as other family snaps. As well there were those inevitable invitation cards, "Your presence is requested etc…." Garden parties, vicarage functions, cocktail parties, hunt balls, and the like.

We sat down talking just as one of the maids came in with tea things, which she put down on a table in front of the fire. It was a typical Scots' meal, the tea itself strong and refreshing, the food plain and heavy on the scones, and small pancakes, delicious and lightly spread with butter and homemade strawberry jam. There was too, wonderful Dundee cake, moist and rich, with walnuts on top. We polished the lot off.

While on the subject, I was once told why the English invented teatime, which was, to fill in that awkward time between lunch, post-luncheon nap, and the cocktail hour. Very sensible.

We all sat around and listened, fascinated, to Jamie recounting tales of his family and friends, and more history of the house, how George Sand had brought Chopin there, who had played for assembled guests, and how Knox had given his first sermon in the chapel, and of course there were ghosts and ghoulies.

We were so comfy in that fire-lit room with the shadows in the corners and the flickering light on Jamie's dear face as he told lurid details about how it was said that an ancestor of dubious character had played cards with the devil and won, and how the infuriated creature had kicked over the marble table on which they had been playing which fell through an arrow embrasure and had fallen, hissing, into the moat, and how when the water was drained in Victorian times and a table with a marble top was found, it had a cloven hoof print seared blackly on its surface. Our shivers were interrupted by the cheerful sound of drinks being made in the pantry. The remainder of the evening before dinner was passed in a similar way, but now with glasses firmly gripped.

We passed several idyllic days with him and with other members of his family who had turned up. This included his new and charming wife Pamela, whose grandfather, I believe it was, founded a famous Indian Army cavalry regiment well-known up and down the Khyber Pass.

We had some great evenings of laughter and food and wine and stories. I found myself drawn to his brother who was visiting and who was an anthropologist, always going off to various parts of the uncivilized world, later with tragic circumstances. News came through of his being abandoned by his guides and bearers in a remote part of Borneo and succumbing on Christmas Eve to starvation. His diary was found near the body giving details to the end.

Eventually we had to pack bags and prepare to leave, but not before we had explored the whole house and its gardens, and the chapel, which had a little museum of the crusaders attached to it, and very hard stone slabs the devout had to kneel on. To this day Scottish Catholicism is taken very seriously.

Vianne and Vicky at Jamie's front door

The time to leave came too soon, and after an interminable train journey we arrived in Glasgow where we were to take a plane for the States.

✳ ✳ ✳ ✳

It was now late summer. We were busy preparing

samples to show to some of our target accounts. I was sensing the possibility of success with some major companies and was working closely with their designers. This was one of the best parts of my job, as they were usually amusing, interesting characters, besides being talented and skilled in their work.

I had been spending the evening with a couple of them and had had much too much to drink. I should have spent the night in a motel but had to be in the studio next day, so chose to drive home. It was warm and the top of the Morgan was down.

I motored at speed through the darkness, headlights shining ahead. It was late and the roads deserted. The Morgan purred along, tyres hissing on the damp road. I never saw the hidden police car. There's nothing quite like the feeling that you get when first you see the red light flickering in your rear view mirror, a combination of panic, anger and deflation.

I slowed, pulled over, and stopped. The trooper walked up, his cruiser still spilling light over the scene. "Holy Toledo, where's the fire?"

"Oh, good evening officer," I always believed in impeccable politeness when dealing with the law. "Was I going too fast?"

"Too fast. Hell, I could hardly catch you. What kind of a car is this anyway? What've you got, a straight eight under that hood?"

I got out and undid the bonnet fasteners. There, in all its glory, was the four-cylinder twin Weber carb DOHC engine steaming in its container.

"Jeez it's tiny." He pushed his Stetson back and stood in an attitude of respectful surprise. "Well I've still got to give you a ticket. You were doin' 90 in a 50-mile-an-hour zone." At that moment his car radio, which was crackling in the background, cackled with an urgent sounding voice. He left me and walked over to pick up and talk into a small radio mike. I saw him nod and say something. He turned to me, "Get in the car. There's an emergency. You'll have to go with me."

I got in and fastened the seat belt. He started the engine and engaged gears. We were off like a rocket. The speedometer climbed, the cruiser seemed to settle on its springs and we careered down the road. I'd heard about the capacity of these police cars, but this was beyond expectation. Apparently they had to be fast in this part of the world to catch the heavily loaded but souped-up jalopies the moonshine runners used to transfer their liquor from the mountain stills to the valley markets.

The cause of all this particular excitement was a bank robbery in nearby Greensboro where my house was. I was, albeit reluctantly, part of a pursuit. Fortunately for me, the excitement was over before it really got going, as a message came through saying the bandit had been apprehended. We reversed direction and returned to my car, where I got a reprimand and a ticket charging me for doing 60 in a 50 mph zone given to me with a wink and a warning.

⁂ ⁂ ⁂ ⁂

I can't remember exactly when it was or why it was that I began to be fearful of heights. I think a seed was planted when I read a short story about a man who couldn't visit his son at school in Switzerland because the establishment was high in the mountains and could only be reached by a precipitous winding road. 'How odd,' I thought. Then I came across a short work by Updike about a man struck suddenly by a phobic fear of crossing high bridges. A strange tale of a phantom hippy guitarist who in a dreamlike state got him over the Tappanzee on the Hudson, north of New York, and then disappeared.

Now, I had never before had any anxieties of this sort, but for some reason I had become fallow ground for the implanting of all sorts of agoraphobic ideas, the culmination of which resulted during a visit by my sister Madeleine and her husband Bob, who lived in the Midwest and had driven down to us in the Carolinas.

One evening after dinner we were talking about this and that and something made Bob remark on Madeleine's behavior as they crossed the Appalachian Mountains in West Virginias, a route I had taken many times myself.

"Yeahh," he said, "she started to blubber and cry and made me stop the car and she lay down in the back and covered herself in a blanket and she moaned and groaned all the way over and down about how fast I was driving and that she felt dizzy and sick. Jeez, she was a real pain in the ass." He said this not unkindly, but with a gentle smile.

"Oh it was awful," she said, and even now her eyes started up teary and moist and her hands trembled and were wet to the touch when I went to comfort her. I thought I had forgotten about the whole business until the time came for us finally to travel to Canada.

I was to go on ahead while Vianne looked after all the really important matters like packing and arranging for movers. All I had to do was find a place to live and take up my duties at the new job. I had gone through a slightly acrimonious leave-taking at my previous place of employment. Most of my fellow workers were happy for me, but the business we were in was highly competitive so management was anxious that I would take formula secrets with me. My assurances to the contrary were viewed with some suspicion.

I had reluctantly sold the Morgan. People who knew said she'll die in Canada. The weather will destroy her. Sell her and get something sensible. I sadly followed this advice and exchanged it, with some monetary adjustments, for a Triumph GT, fast and sleek but comfortable and weatherproof. The car was a fastback so could accept a lot more stuff than could the Morgan. We loaded up one sunny autumn morning.

Tearful leave-taking followed. Vicky couldn't figure out why I couldn't take her with me. My heart melted. I felt awful, but I finally left, watching them get smaller in the rear view mirror as I drove away. Depression lasted until I hit the suburbs of Greensboro and I hit the open road. My spirits lifted as the car got into its stride and growled away up the highway to a new life in a new country.

Other than stopping for lunch in a small roadside eatery in West Virginia, where the waitress, with an elaborate hairstyle, high and convoluted, asked, while chewing gum, if I wanted congealed salad with my burger, I kept up a steady pace so that I reached my first objective, which was Louisville Kentucky, late in the evening.

The next morning I reported to the headquarters of the American corporation that owned the company I was to work with in Canada, spending the day in meetings with chemists who formulated the products I was to use in making furniture look more glamorous, and with sales, public relations, and advertising departments who were to help me in my task. I left in the early evening, meaning to get as far as Cincinnati, where I would spend the night. I was to regret that decision.

An hour or two later as I breasted a hill, I saw, laid

out before and below me, the glittering lights of a large city. I thought 'Goody, a couple of dry martinis, a steak with all the trimmings, apple pie and bed.' Tired, aching and slightly light-headed, I started to look for a motel. The highway swooped down the hill and what with the heavy and fast traffic which seemed to be carrying me along with it and the alarming sensation of being high above the lights below, I began to sweat and shake.

A strange panicky feeling came over me. Then I saw the bridge. It was slightly below my line of sight, but I could tell that it was high, long, and gigantic. Its cantilevered girders stretched up and up. The road I was on would go right over it and I knew that in my present state, I would not be able to follow.

I had been much impressed by a film seen when I was a child in the thirties. It was about a young English officer who, when his regiment was ordered to the Sudan to war, resigned his commission through fear. It was called "The Four Feathers." He had remarked to a friend that he had felt fate closing in on him remorselessly and implacably. I felt the same way, as though all the elements of disaster and other horrors were waiting in the shadows to pounce.

Thankfully there was an exit to a service road ahead, so I left the highway and pulled up, sweating and shaking. I lit a cigarette and swigged scotch from the flask.

'God. What's going on?' The feelings of weakness,

fear and general dismay were almost too much to bear. Although I didn't know it then, I was, of course, having my first, full-blown panic attack, brought on by my new fear of heights.

As I calmed down, I took stock of my situation. Looking up I could now see the bridge arcing away into the night sky. I seemed to be on a quiet riverside road. I could tell from the cars lights that this was a two-tier structure, the southbound traffic on the higher level and the northbound on the lower. Well that was better than the other way round, I thought. I've got to cross somehow.

'Come on, pull yourself together. Easier at night when you can't see as much than in the broad light of day when all is revealed. okay. I took another swig for false courage and off we went.

I found the way back up the hill and rejoined the hurrying cars and trucks. I worked my way into a centre lane, gripped the wheel, and stared straight ahead at the car in front. I was over in a whirl of lights and sound and noise. The road stretched away up the hill. A sign flashed by. It said, "Welcome to the Hoosier State." This was Indiana. The next sign I saw, with infinite gratitude, said "Holiday Inn." I really enjoyed my martinis that night.

Still feeling a bit shaky from the previous night's experience, I had breakfast the next morning, checked out, and pointed myself north. Mile after interminable mile followed. I figured I could make London, Ontario, where my firm was based, that night, so kept up a good pace and managed to reach the southern end of Detroit by late afternoon.

A gloomy, wet, misty day had deteriorated into an even worse evening, and somehow I had missed a turn or taken a wrong one, but whatever the reason, I realized I was not still on the main highway and was in fact driving through what looked like a very dodgy neighbourhood.

Shadows flitted by at traffic lights, cheap looking bars and cafés garishly proclaimed their dubious wares. I felt very uneasy at the hostility of the looks I was getting at stop signs, but had to somehow find my way back to the right road, so rolled down the window and addressed two black youths who were leaning against the light standard at the corner.

"Can you help me?" I asked? They slouched over to the car, their hands in pockets, their faces indicating incredulous disbelief.

"Are you for real? Jesus Christ. What's a Honky doing in this neighbourhood?"

"Well, er, I think I'm lost," I said.

"You sure as hell are. You a Limey? Yeah, okay. We'll help then." This was not the first time my nationality had saved my bacon in this country. "okay, here's what you do." As he described the route I should take, I noticed the little group was getting bigger and some of the looks were getting blacker, and I mean that in the literary sense. I was relieved to be on my way again and it was only when I had turned several corners and was obviously on the right track that I felt secure.

It was then that I noticed a sign that proclaimed, "Bridge To Canada" ahead, and then, almost immediately, I saw this monstrous structure looming like a prehistoric mammoth in the swirling fog. My heart sank. My arms turned to jelly. I felt physically sick. What was I to do? I knew I couldn't drive onto it. I might cause an accident. I might faint.

"Turn at next exit for Tunnel to Canada," said another sign. Talk about the nick of time. I steered to the right, following the cars ahead, and came to a stop at a booth with a man in uniform. I felt like kissing him. I didn't think I was frightened of tunnels but, just in case, I took a drink from the faithful flask and, singing "Rule Britannia" at the top of my voice, descended into a brightly lit tunnel lined with white tiles. 'Rather like a public lavatory,' I thought.

At the other end, at another booth, was another uniformed man, but there was something different here. There was something different about the whole scene. First the guard called me "Sir" and wished me a good evening and "Welcome to Canada." There was politeness here. Secondly, after the flag I had got so used to seeing, the Stars and Stripes, handsome as they no doubt are, it was somehow uplifting to see something different, if strange, red and white with a maple leaf emblem. But wait, there was another flag, red, with what looked like an armorial bearing on it, and, 'Oh joy, what was this?' In the corner, my flag, the crosses of the Union Jack, Britain's ensign. I was enveloped in goose bumps and almost burst into tears. Though the years in America had, on the whole, been happy, I had still been an exile there. Here, I felt I had come home.

The next hour or so was spent filling up forms and being interviewed. I noticed with pleasure, the total absence of weaponry. None of the officials seemed armed. I was entering the country with a temporary visa. Though most details had already been cleared, I was virtually accepted by reason of my nationality as an Englishman. I was entering as a member of the Commonwealth and was thus already in the family, so to speak.

In no time I was driving through the city of Windsor. Looking about me with interest, the streets looked tidier and cleaner, the buildings seemed more substantial and less burdened with illuminated advertising signs. The streets were certainly more populated than in Detroit for this time of night and it seemed strange to see that most faces were white. How odd. I had got so used to seeing either predominately black people in downtown America at night, or streets that were totally empty, most of the white citizens having abandoned the centre of town for the suburbs.

As I started to clear the outskirts and enter the countryside, I was struck by the total lack of highway advertising billboards. What a relief. The countryside appeared completely untrammeled by anything other than appurtenances of an agricultural nature. The rest was fields, woods, farmhouses and, of course, barns. It was quite dark by this time, but the impression I was forming was certainly favourable. It all reminded me faintly of England.

I reached London and checked into a motel. Completely exhausted, I fell into bed without dinner or a drink. I slept without moving until banging on the door brought me out of my deep sleep. Dragging on a robe, I opened the door to see a fresh-faced young man standing on the step.

"Good morning. I'm Bob Rogers. Welcome to London. Have you had breakfast?"

The next few days were spent getting oriented with work and with workmates. Everyone was friendly and helpful with the exception of a very arrogant Swiss who was, it seems, my chief chemist. I knew I would have trouble with him. The young man I had met earlier had been assigned by my boss to look after me, show me around, and find me a place to live. I spent many amenable evenings with him and we became good friends.

I next had a meeting with all my sales people and with the staff who worked in the colour styling studio. Business wasn't exactly booming. The competition was stiff, and one of the reasons I had been hired was to try to improve the picture and get more new accounts. Time flew by as it does when one is busy and life is interesting.

✳ ✳ ✳ ✳

November came and went. Vianne and Vicky arrived. Life was sweet. They both loved it here and we looked forward to a future that appeared rosy. We moved into a small neat modern flat in town. It was our first taste of apartment block living and we rather enjoyed it. Everything worked, and it was nice to have no janitorial worries to have to cope with. My boss had promised, as part of the employment deal, that the company would help me to find a permanent residence, and Vianne and I had dreams of living in the country, so this period was to be strictly temporary.

We had our first taste of Canada's winter at Christmas time. It came fast, stayed long, and was quite brutal. After a couple of experiences on the open road in blizzard-like conditions, once during the day in a white-out when I didn't know which side of the road I was on and didn't dare stop as it was a busy two-lane highway and finished in the ditch on the wrong side of the road facing backwards, and once in the same conditions except it was pitch dark at night, I decided that life could end abruptly here and that I had better be very careful at all times.

I heard Vianne once telling her mum on the phone, "Mamma, the snow goes sideways here." But in spite of this, we really were enjoying life and work. And in spite of the negative side of winter, it could be quite beautiful.

The elemental, savage aspect of it was, somehow appealing, and inspired me to write about it, and of course, to paint it.

I was fascinated by the ever-present little birds that appeared as soon as snow began to blow and drift across the highway like a cold surf on a beach, the way heavily drifted snow marbled and sculpted by the winds reminded me of parts of the Sudanese desert, and how the effect of a sudden shift in wind direction or a cessation of storm would cause the clouds to disappear or part, revealing the most brilliant multi-coloured streaks across the western horizon, bathing the surrounding countryside with technicolour madness.

* * * *

Spring, or at least one mild day in March came. We, in our naiveté, thought it was the real thing, and rushed out to explore. We drove north and west and came to the coast of Lake Huron. The edge of the lake was marked by tumbled piles of ice. In the far distance one could just see a smoky horizon where the open water was. spring suddenly seemed very far away again.

We drove home, our spirits slightly dampened, especially as it clouded up again and began to snow as we reached our little flat in London. Milder weather did finally arrive and in time trees budded, fields began to green up, and skies became a softer blue. The long drives I had to make to attend all the customers we serviced were enjoyable and varied.

The countryside was not dramatic in any way but was pleasant and rolling, intensively farmed with fields, larger than England's, roughly hedged like parts of East Anglia and which reminded me of home a bit. There were other odd similarities. They called it the "railway" here not "railroad" as in America. The spellings retained the letter "u" which the Americans had discarded in words like "honour," "harbour," "colour." This was to me reassuring. The signs said "County Perth." In England it was "The County of so-and-so...." The Yanks did it backwards. I know this must seem silly to some, but to me it was heaven.

Also this part of Ontario was full of expatriates from the UK, and the grocery and liquor stores stocked Cross and Blackwell's mayonnaise, Melton Mowbray Pies, various English beers, anchovy paste, and fish paste for eating with bread and butter and oh, be still my heart, Lyle's

Golden Syrup, that most decadent of spreads that satisfied sweet tooths from Bombay to Brisbane.

✳ ✳ ✳ ✳

Vianne and I had decided that we wanted to live in the country, so she spent time driving around with Vicky exploring and looking for sale signs. We had noticed some really handsome old houses, some abandoned, that we thought we could fix up. Alas, we were discouraged by those who would be advancing the cash, but we were so excited at the thought of living the life of the country gentleman and chatelaine that no amount of gloomy advice would put us off our goal.

We spent hours planning. We would buy a second hand Land Rover for sure, and green Wellies and lots of old furniture. We couldn't afford antiques, but my job had taught me to conjure up quite realistic reproductions. Given a file and clinker pieces and some stains, rags, and a brush, no one would know the difference.

One day I was driving to a prospective customer in a town called Stratford. On the way, I took a wrong turn and finished up going through some really pretty country, rolling hills, streams, and wooded heights. The farms I passed were all neat and tidy. The fields well husbanded, the black and white cows looked contented and placid as they stood knee deep in long lush grass. Then came a bend in the road, a steep hill, and I was entering the town of St. Mary's. There had been a short but heavy downpour and it was at this moment that the clouds parted, the rains stopped and the view below was bathed in brilliant light.

The buildings were made of a pale coloured stone and seemed almost ethereal, though the architecture was strong and robust. The scene had the quality of a watercolour. The windows and doorways were handsome with transoms, lunettes and rooflines in the Scottish, English, and Irish vernacular. The whole town looked very Scottish in fact, and reminded me very much of Invergordon. I decided there and then that Vianne should come here soon to see the place. I was convinced she would like it as much as I did.

I had met through work, a designer who was well known internationally and who was working with one of our customers. He and I hit it off right away and that weekend, Vianne and I had been invited to his cottage for lunch and to meet his family. The route went through St. Mary's, so Vianne was able to see this pretty town for herself. She became as besotted as I was and we decided that this was the area in which we wanted to live.

The lunch turned out to be a success on all fronts. We all liked each other. The food was marvelous, so was the wine, but the most memorable part was the house itself, made of fieldstone, a local building material, great heavy slabs of granite-like stone rough-hewn and of a textural and colour quality that immediately captivated us. The colours were delicate with subtle tones of blue, grey, pink, and grey green.

This particular house was a single storey structure and dated from the 1880s. Deep windows, handsome chimneys, well-proportioned doors and dark grey roof of black tile revealed its origin, a typical crofter's highland habitat, Cromarty or Ross, the northeasterly Highlands. On the way home we excitedly made plans to find one for us just like it.

One day, I was working on a conveyor line at one of our customers' factories. It was hot and it was humid and I was unhappy because the samples we were working on were not coming out looking anything like the original samples we had submitted. The principals of thc company had been out to see how we were getting on and had left displeased. The pressure was on. I had to make decisions. The others looked at me. The line was stopped. I wanted the floor to swallow me up when my name was called over the loudspeaker. There was a telephone call for me. I told the lads what to do to try to alter the colour, a technique that sometimes worked and sometimes didn't, called shading, and left to find the nearest telephone.

It was Vianne. She said, "You'd better start looking for a secondhand Land Rover. I think I've found thc perfect place. Can you get out early to come and look? It's just outside St. Marys." I got back to the line to find that they had managed to cobble up the finish sufficiently that I felt I could sell it to the powers-that-be next day. It was now almost closing time for the plant so I stole away, got in the car and left for home.

I met Vi and Vicky and we drove to St. Mary's. It was a lovely warm evening in mid-May. We left the main road and followed a gravel lane that followed the course of a little stream. It was all very rustic and charming, the stream lined with willow, bulrushes, and reeds. It splashed and gurgled, sparkling and rippling as it broke and foamed over the rocks and stones. As we cleared a line of trees, to our left the house came into view. I held my breath.

This was extraordinary. It was a miniature replica of Haddiscoe Hall, my grandfather's house in England where I had spent my youth during the war. The design was Georgian, made of fieldstone. It was set against a hill with majestic trees forming a half circle around its back, acting as a sort of backdrop. We got out of the car and walked towards it.

There was smoke coming from one of its many chimneys. We learnt that it was rented out to farm workers who occupied part of the building. Vicky had gone hurtling off around the back and we followed her. The building was two storey in the front and single at the back, as it, in effect, climbed the hill. It had to be the prettiest house I had ever seen.

I resolved we would buy it if my new boss Tom and the company financed it for me. As it happened, he did, under the most generous of terms. He really was the nicest man with enormous interests in all sorts of subjects. He was keenly aware of the more attractive aspects of life, travel, food, and wine. His wife was a pretty Danish girl who shared his interests and was obviously besotted with him. I was to spend twenty happy years working with him and occasionally playing. They loved to party and socialize and were always inclusive where we were concerned. His mum was a dear too, and would have us over for delicious dinners.

❋ ❋ ❋ ❋

It took about three weeks to settle all the details and then the magic day came that saw us moving, unpacking, and examining what we had in more detail. A cursory inspection with experts had revealed a well-built and reasonably well-looked-after house with no structural faults, but a lot of work would be needed as far as interior decorating was concerned. The floors were a sea of linoleum and the walls hideous with cabbage rose wallpaper. There were four fireplaces all bricked up, though there were seven chimneys all told, which was interesting.

The biggest surprise of all came when we had some friends over later in the month to help strip paper and rip up lino. One of the young men who worked in my studio had discovered the attic and had shinnied up a ladder to explore it, followed by a couple of others. Suddenly, there came loud yelling and shouting and down the ladder came a chest, a sea chest. It was lowered gently to the floor and opened.

It was like Aladdin's fable, except instead of jewels and gold, here we had books, leather-bound, and books wrapped in what looked like canvas and which turned out to be sailcloth. Fabulous charts printed in the 1840s on which were pencil markings and notes denoting positions at sea. These told the history of the voyages. There was a tiny hole where the compass point had broken the paper. Date, time, latitude and longitude. The ships were barques and schooners. All the charts showed that this sailor had circumnavigated the world and had rounded both capes. His papers and letters indicated that he had seen the exotic and the ordinary. He had carried in his ship, salted beef from New Orleans, Guano fertilizer from Peru, and mixed cargo to Europe and back to the Indies with cotton from the Mills of Lancashire.

Other notes and diaries demonstrated his skills as an amateur doctor, for the ship didn't carry an actual one. There were some interesting cures and hints for temporary use during emergencies, some bizarre recommendations for relief of piles, which must have been both embarrassing and uncomfortable as it involved some heavy applications of sheep's feces to the affected area, presumably by the captain.

There were pictures, clothes, and china. We had just finished gasping when more chests came down similarly filled. Then there was furniture, chairs, tables, lamps, and cupboards, all antique and all perfect for the house. The pictures were mostly paintings and photographs of the family. The whole collection was quite extraordinary, unique and probably quite valuable.

We spent all our spare time and all our spare cash working on improving the inside, sanding floors, painting walls, opening fireplaces. We had a furnace. A new heating system installed. Stoves and refrigerators arrived and were hooked up. Broken windows were replaced. Chimneys were cleaned by a lovely man who wore a tattered top hat and evening suit in the old style of chimney sweeps. Milk, butter, eggs, and light groceries were delivered by a red-cheeked local who whistled and wore a blue striped apron. It was all as though time had never happened and we were back in the 1930s. We loved it.

Neighbours came by and offered help and told us stories of the house and its inhabitants and its ghosts. The latter subject was made much of by one of the visitors who seemed to know a good deal about the previous family, its origins and its peculiarities. He and his wife became very close to us in the ensuing years and we were to enjoy many happy times together. They were lovely, warm, generous and openhearted people.

Others came to us offering help and advice. Everyone was perfectly marvelous in every way and some families adopted us *en masse*. We were included in family matters including magical Christmases with masses of children and animals. Friendship was, with these, as a precious gem.

Summer passed happily. The days were long, the air sweet and refreshing, the nights awe-inspiring with the deep velvety skies brilliant with stars and silence. We loved, worked, played, and thanked the powers that be for the blessings bestowed.

I needed a long ladder to do some work on the guttering of the house, so went to borrow one from a neighbour. This one was a dairy farmer who would one day rent my land for his cattle to graze. He was a spare, tall, laconic man with a dry sense of humour. We were standing together chatting. I said, looking down into the valley in which my house was situated, "God, this is such a beautiful spot Don, I can't believe I'm here. It's like a dream."

"Wait 'til the fuckin' winter arrives," he growled. I took the ladder and left.

❋ ❋ ❋ ❋

The autumn came and was lovely. The colours of the various trees were spectacular and we enjoyed the county fairs with their jam competitions, flower and vegetable displays, rose shows, parades, fairs, fetes, and all the other celebratory occasions of harvest-time. People smiled and were content.

Then the wind shifted to the north and all the leaves, stalks, twigs and other detritus of the countryside were blown into motion. In the towns and villages, empty paper coffee cups, newspapers, and a hundred and one other articles of temporary attachment were sent fluttering and forlorn into used car lots and doorways and greying gardens. Cold dust, gritty and sharp, made the eyes blink, hurt, and water. There was an ominous coppery grey in the clouds on the northern horizon. I remembered the farmer's comment.

Actually the months of November and December were not too alarming. It was as though we were being lulled into a state of false security.

❋ ❋ ❋ ❋

The day before Christmas Eve, I was working in my studio in London when my phone rang. It was Vianne. "You'd better get home. There's a storm coming with tons of snow. I'm worried." It was three in the afternoon and the sun was shining in London but I'd heard about these storms off the lakes and how fast they could move and change conditions, so assuring her that I was on my way, I donned coat and gloves and got into the car.

As I was clearing the northern suburbs I could see ahead the sky, though blue and innocuous overhead, had become indistinct and white ahead. Then specks of snow began to rattle on the hood and windshield.

I noticed parenthetically, out of the corner of my eye, tiny birds diving to the ground pecking at the gravel and swooping back into the whirling mists. They seemed to be trying to keep up with me, rather like dolphins do with a ship in the tropics.

Then, with a swoosh, the car was swallowed up in a white cloud of howling sound. The car rocked and trembled as it tried to keep in motion against the moving rushing waves of wind. All the familiar objects of the roadside disappeared. The telegraph poles, wire fences, grass verges, they were no more. The wipers flailed miserably and unsuccessfully against the icy build-up on the glass. I braked and slowed to a crawl. I could barely see the front of the hood.

Ah, thank God. A red light flickered ahead. I followed the light and the tracks, and then noticed behind me, headlights following. This was better. I was in a convoy. I was being introduced to that Canadian winter horror, the white-out.

It was now getting dark. I glanced at my watch. My God, it was five-thirty. We had been struggling for nearly two hours. Up ahead it seemed to be clearer. Yes, I could see the vehicle, a pick-up truck. I looked back. There was a sedan with a very pale driver, like me, probably a commuter.

Suddenly the snow stopped almost completely. All the familiar landmarks were back. What a feeling of relief. I ached and felt sweaty and longed for home, family, a hot bath, and a stiff drink, not necessarily in that order. I came to the Rannoch corner and started down the road that led to my house. The snow had drifted in great swathes at angles across the road. The car shuddered as it hit them and snow flew up in great clouds.

Now it was dark. Down the hill across Flat Creek, brake, gear down to second. Here was the entry to the drive that meandered along the winding frozen stream to home, warmth, comfort, lights and love. Thump. Car stops dead.

Engine stalls. Turn key. Rev up. Engage clutch. Lurch forward about an inch and the tyres scream in protest on the ice. Ahead, a white wall. An impenetrable curtain.

The wind starts to howl again. The lane has drifts across it. I'm stuck in one. Got to walk. The lane is about a quarter of a mile long. I'm in a business suit with thin city shoes, gloves and scarf more suitable for a quick run to an urban restaurant for lunch, certainly not for these conditions. I'm also carrying bags of groceries, cigarettes and gin.

I started to walk or rather, stumble, down the drive. Some drifts were waist high. I fell several times, then I saw the lights, I thought, for some reason, about the title of an old German UFA film I had seen as a child about Arctic exploration, The White Hell of Pitz Palu. It seemed somehow, appropriate.

I had to step down into the house. The snow outside was higher by some several feet than the floor inside. Vi and Vicky hugged me and we all started talking at the same time. They had had a dreadful time. Vicky had been sick. They were running out of food and Vianne had just smoked her last cigarette. Her sense of humour was about to desert her. Gin was also getting dangerously low. The furnace, thank God was still working away. We drank several martinis, had a cozy dinner by the fire, tucked Vicky into bed, and went to our room and cuddled together all night. It had been a long day.

Hookway farm. The storm of 1970.

⁂ ⁂ ⁂ ⁂

Winter, which seemed to go on forever, finally, one magical day in late February, seemed to be releasing its grip. A watery sun peered down on us and the sound of dripping water was everywhere. The snow was now threadbare and felt punky when trod on. We sat outside and watched Vicky running around. The sun, though weak, had a little warmth. We relished the change.

In our innocence we didn't realize that this was a false dawn. That night the wind shifted to the north and howled at the house, hurling snow and hail that rattled on the tin roof above, its elemental fury frightening in its intensity. It reminded me of those nights in the north Atlantic during the war when I was trying to keep my dinner down.

⁂ ⁂ ⁂ ⁂

Besides the miseries, we did have some wonderful times in the winter. Parties were common and the adventure of fighting one's way through blizzards to get to them was an experience in itself. How we survived some of these jaunts is beyond me, especially the return journey when slightly under the weather.

We gave some astounding gatherings of our own. They were known locally as "Payne's Thrashes," and consisted of hordes of people, some of whom we didn't know from Adam, drinking copious amounts of booze, dancing, flirting, and filling every room with laughter and talk and generally raising the roof. Negotiating the narrow lane after the party, back to the highway, sometimes all the way in reverse with people holding lights to mark the tricky bits, was, as well, a specialty of our parties noted by the attendees with some apprehension.

⁂ ⁂ ⁂ ⁂

Well, the cold did finally let go, and the thaw really did set in, and the stream swelled to become a river that splashed and gurgled and overwhelmed the banks, and the world became green again. We opened windows and explored all the places and parts we couldn't get to during the snows. Our barn cats, that had adopted us, presented us with mewling tiny bundles of untidy damp kittens that grew and frolicked. We had been given also, two Labrador crosses as puppies, and they all slept together with the cats in the straw in the barn.

The heartbreakingly short Ontario spring came and went. One day, cool, fresh, and utterly delightful, the next hot, humid breathless and sapping of strength. We languished in perspiring discomfort and thought longingly of cold December nights. Strange, this climate. We made friends with the neighbouring farmers and would spend time in their curiously cool messy kitchens drinking cold beer and listening to tales of past winters, cold comforts, calamitous farm prices, and other matters of import in the agricultural world.

* * * *

A strange thing happened one day. I had started to clear the ground in front of the house meaning to plant grass seed for a lawn and a flowerbed for perennials. I had drawn all the plans. It was going to be a miniature Haddiscoe, the house in which I had spent my teenage years, and which had a wonderful and extensive garden. I was just standing, resting on my hoe and looking up at the house and dreaming, when, as if in a timeless flash, I was aware of someone looking at me, or no, looking at us, me and the house.

There were two old ladies in black standing next to me, gazing at the house. "Hello. We hoped we didn't startle you. We used to live here when we were children. Would it be alright if we looked around?"

"Of course," I said, getting over the initial shock that their sudden appearance had caused. "Please do come in."

They both were heavily dressed considering the heat of the day, but seemed quite at ease. Their little faces were pink with rosy cheeks. Did they have hats? I can't remember. They looked old-fashioned and walked with small mincing steps. We went into the house. Vi wasn't home. Vicky was at school. I was alone.

We went upstairs. They had been relatively reticent while they looked around, up until the moment that they saw the pictures that we had found in the attic and which we had grouped together with some of my military prints.

"Oh look," they said, "there's Grandpa Hookway and there's Aunt Amy and, oh dear, there's Granmama Netta." They became quite animated as they discovered various relatives. "We don't know who they are," they said disapprovingly, pointing at the soldier prints.

"Would you like tea?" I asked.

"No, we can't stay, thank you. Come along Doris."

"But you've only seen part of the house."

"No, we must go. You seem quite happy here. This is comforting for us to see." We went down and out into the bright sunshine and walked down to where they had parked their car. It was a big old black Packard, 1950s vintage. As it drove away they didn't wave.

Thus began the incidents that would come and go and lead us to believing that some sort of supernatural activity was taking place here. The Haunting of Hookway Farm.

* * * *

Perhaps I will gather all the peculiarly interesting stories of things strange that happened to me and mine and to friends here, so as there might be more continuity.

The oddest things happened. These all happened over a span of some years. I don't believe what I was told when a child, living from time to time in old houses and visiting very old houses, that if you wanted there to be a ghost, there would be one. Bizarre really. I'm much too timid to want to be scared, and sometimes I was. Perhaps too vivid an imagination could be blamed. Possibly, creaks and groans of settling floors, tree branches scratching outer walls in winds, can really stir those of us that are sensitive and impressionable.

My friend Jamie told me once of visiting an old school chum who lived in an older block of flats in west London in the fifties. He arrived early before his friend came home from work, but he had a key so let himself in. He raided the fridge and settled down with a book from the well-stocked library, then fell asleep. He was woken by the sound of some sort of machinery rattling and banging outside in the hall. Silence. Then a really loud crash followed by the commotion of voices raised in urgency and alarm. Then silence again. He went to the front door and peered out. The landing was deserted. He went back to his nap.

Later, having a drink with his pal, he mentioned the noise he had heard, to be told that today was the anniversary of a tragedy that befell an ancient elevator that used to clank its way up and down between the stairs during Victorian times. Apparently this was not the first time the phenomenon had been heard. So houses did not have to be crumbling old ruins nor did incidents of the paranormal have to occur during the hours of darkness.

Some time in the late thirties the BBC did a program about the subject that was very popular and kept half the population of the country awake most of the night. Part of the show, the highlight really, was when they broadcast from the most haunted house in England, an old vicarage in Suffolk called Borley Rectory. They set up all the equipment in the cellar. The announcer, whose name I can't remember, but who was well known and usually read the nine o'clock news, sat alone with all his paraphernalia, except for his dog. The thought here was that dogs are unusually sensitive to the presence of spiritual communicants.

It was a warm summer night. The compere kept up a running commentary of what was happening, or rather what wasn't happening, for nothing at all had taken place so far. Things, however were about to get more lively. Appropriately, at about midnight, Fido who had been fast asleep in a basket, woke up and growled, the hair on his back, reported the BBC man, standing at full attention. The temperature suddenly dropped by some measurable degree, and a strong perfume of, I think it was oleander or something of that sort, filled the cellar. I believe the BBC chap packed up and went home rather shaken shortly afterwards.

Some years later, when between wives, I gave a small dinner party for a lovely English actress I knew who brought some friends. One was an elderly Brit who was in the Stratford Shakespearean Festival company, and who pranced into the house announcing in a loud voice that he had decided not to put a pot to flame that night but to eat at Teddy's. He asked me later if I was gay and, when answered in the negative, said "Pity." The other guests were a couple who seemed quite innocuous and uninteresting. I wondered why they had been brought. The usual progression of drinks, polite conversation, and dinner ensued.

The room, which I had always loved, was long and low and had a fire which popped and glowed at one end, casting flickering shadows that reached where we sat at an old heavy pine table covered with the remains of food, spluttering candles, and empty wine bottles, the dogs, asleep underneath. We sipped brandy and waxed philosophical.

The chat here too, turned to the subject of the supernatural, and that's when the fun started. It turned out that the husband was a defrocked priest and the wife a clairvoyant. She could, and often did carry out exorcisms. She could see auras of course, and professionally exercised all these gifts with some regularity.

She had, in fact, just finished a job where she had exorcised a farmhouse in the Hockley Valley, north of Toronto. She told us all about it now. The point I want to make here is that however strange, bizarre, and even slightly ridiculous her stories were, she herself was utterly believable.

She was a motherly-looking, not terribly attractive, mousy sort of person, modest and quiet. The story went something like this. A friend had bought this century-old house and had been unable to live in it because of all the strange and frightening things that were going on, noises, breaking plates and glassware, apparitions, the lot. Our exorcist was called in for help. She spent a week there alone. Nothing happened until the seventh day when she was having a nap in the afternoon. Something woke her.

There was a figure of a man standing at the foot of the bed looking at her. Apparently these people communicate with spirits not by speech but by thought exchange. In the process it came about that this person had been killed by his wife. She gave him small doses of poison every day until, at the end, just before he expired, he sat up and said to her: "I know what you've done," and died. She then went potty, took a fatal dose herself and went to her reward.

When questioned about his present disinclination to join her in the beyond, he said that there was only one person he now trusted to take him, and that was his father, but he couldn't reach him to get his help to go to the next stage or station or whatever, so she, the medium, summoned dad from the beyond, got them together and off they went. Case closed. House now livable.

Extraordinary.

She told us about other hair-raising matters. He, the ex-priest, told of some of his exploits, and we simmered gently into the night. More brandy. The fire continued to snap and send the odd spark onto the worn out carpet. She then said, looking at me meaningfully, "You know of course Teddy, that this house is haunted."

This was interesting but unwelcome news as I was living alone at the time. We did know certain things about the house and its occupants over the last hundred years, involving a certain room at the back of the house that the dogs wouldn't go into and that Vicky couldn't sleep in when we had visitors who took her room. The light was ugly and cold as it glared in from the north. We never liked the room, and usually used it as a spare for visitors in the hope that they wouldn't notice any untoward events.

In any event, she got up and said, "Here, I'll tell you where the centre of abnormal activity is." I reluctantly followed her to this room. She described the events that had taken place in the 1870s: a story of loneliness and malice, of misery and hatred, and there was more, but I stopped her. I didn't want to know more. We had had twenty happy years there and I wanted nothing to spoil those times.

We returned to the dining room and its warmth and cozy friendliness. She then regaled us with bizarre tales of being trained in improving her gifts of aura sight, how her teacher warned her and her girl friend of many years, who had the same talents, never to practice the exercises prescribed under anything but electric light or daylight, never, under any circumstances, to do them by candle light, etc. Of course, being young and foolish, they disobeyed, and in one terrifying moment her friend turned first into a man, then into a wolf. Six months later she became a lesbian and six months after that tried to kill her.

⁂ ⁂ ⁂ ⁂

Life had become dichotomous for me, the major part of it at the studio or office or on the road or in some factory, the minor, but more precious time, at home with family, friends, and the house and garden. Bizarre, comical, and sometimes sad and tragic things occurred from time to time that kept us amused and occasionally humbled.

One night the dairy cows that meandered through the fields we rented to our neighbour farmer, broke through the fence and we woke and breakfasted with them looking through our dining room window, chewing contentedly as though guests at our table. The holes they made in my beautiful lawn did not however, amuse me.

One early summer evening we helped the same farmer find lost small heifers that had wandered into our bush. There was a strange, almost magical experience with fireflies sparkling around our heads, the undergrowth crackling under our feet, the calling to each other as we stumbled about in the darkening woods, getting lost and not minding it. The warmth and the scents of wild flowers and fresh grass pressed by clumsy feet. The capturing of nervous beasts and then all collecting in the farmer's kitchen to tell tall stories and drink homemade cider. Later to sleep happily in dry crisp sheets feeling as though one had accomplished something real and not unimportant.

One morning, we got up to discover the river running high, the lane impassable, with the only way to our cars parked at the road end of the drive through our neighbour's farm situated above us on the top of the hill. Subsequently we negotiated the orchard, the muddy lane to the milking barn, walking the full length of the barn with all the early morning activity of the dairy process going on around us, together with the scents of hay, cream, fodder, urine, and excreta all somehow blending to make that wonderful redolence that is the farm yard, with us struggling in thin shoes, raincoats and city clothes with papers, portfolios, and briefcase, out of the barn and down the hill to the cars. The rain was coming down in sheets.

Other even less palatable aspects of the life rural, especially for the transplanted urbanite, is in the tooth and claw department. Accidents happen everywhere but in the middle of nowhere, or in the winter, one is dependent largely on one's own capacity to cope. Dispatching an animal that was hurt, or a bird that had lost its ability to fly, or any of a hundred things that can happen, can be a traumatic experience.

One evening we were sitting having martinis with friends from Detroit when an obviously rabid raccoon staggered across our lawn. We couldn't handle this. I had never obtained a rifle, though in retrospect, I should have. I called a neighbour who said he would be right down. He sounded tipsy on the phone. I thought, 'Oh well, so was I.'

Down the lane comes a cloud of dust. Flying it was! A bright red truck emerged and came to a screaming stop. From dust and truck appears friend from next door, rifle over shoulder,. Our friends from Detroit, who are highly sophisticated attorneys, very chic and very civilized, are looking a little alarmed at this point. Wife and I, somewhat bemused. Raccoon climbs tree, rifle goes to shoulder, shot fired, poor critter drops to ground, salutations all round, we go in for dinner somewhat chastened.

Another one. It's the middle of the night, in the middle of winter, in the middle of a howling blizzard and I'm woken by a faint voice crying outside. The wind makes it almost impossible to hear, but it does get me out of bed and to the window to peer out and barely see someone out there at the front door. What is really alarming is that the reason I can see him at all in this blinding snowstorm, is because his figure is illuminated by a fire that is blazing down by the drive shed. Shit. What the hell is going on? Vi's awake. So is Vicky. We run around. I go down and let this half frozen Samaritan in. He had been driving to an early shift in St. Mary's and saw the fire.

I called the local brigade. Vi made the man hot tea. I then, still in pajamas and slippers, rushed and fell and slipped and slid through the snow and ice down to where the cars were parked near the conflagration. In my panicky state I fumbled with the key to start. Of course it wouldn't. It was too cold. Finally though, I got it going and moved it further away. Then back to the other one. That was even more troublesome. Finally all was done and I stumbled back to the house.

I had by now realized what had happened. We had workmen renovating the sheds and they had had a brazier going for the work. When they left for the night they thought they had doused the fire. They hadn't, and the increasing wind had started it again and had then blown the drum over. If this wonderful man hadn't warned us, the sheds would have gone, then the giant barn, and then perhaps a spark to the house carried by the wind, then perhaps disaster.

The firemen had now arrived and I was standing with some other neighbours who had seen the flames and had come to help, when suddenly there was a little commotion from a nearby group and I heard a coughing, choking sound. A figure detached itself from the gathering and fell like a log to the ground. I rushed over. It was the Good Samaritan. He was dead. It transpired afterwards that he had a heart condition and that this incident had brought on a massive attack. It was very difficult to attend the funeral.

✵ ✵ ✵ ✵

It was about this time that I received word that my father, Cecil, had died. We had never got on very well, though there had been some exceptions. When I was little, he used to tell me stories of the trenches in the First World War and show me his maps and revolver and draw little pictures of soldiers of the time. He had gone to France in early 1916 just in time for the slaughter on the Somme. He went over the top with his regiment, the Royal Scots Fusiliers. He was 19 and had only left school and Sandhurst Military Academy the year before, basically still a schoolboy.

Now a second lieutenant, stumbling through the barbed wire and mud, gun in one hand, walking stick in the other, six foot five tall, the tallest man in the regiment except for the piper, who preceded him and his men. Of course the German machine gunners couldn't miss them and he soon fell, shot through the ankle. The piper, not so lucky, mortally hit, dropped in mid chant.

I believe the British Army alone lost 60,000 men between six a.m. and noon, the losses of the best and bravest and youngest to be felt then and later in 1939 when we had to face the Germans again without them.

My father had to spend the night in a shell hole, where he had dragged himself, and which he had to share with a wounded German who snored all night. He was rescued by stretcher-bearers next day and sent back to England to recuperate, and where Lovell, his brother, said to him, "Jesus Christ Cecil, the ankle! What were you doing, walking on your fucking hands?"

While showing me his wartime paraphernalia, he would tell me funny stories, and let me wear his Glengarry cap, blue with diced red and white along the sides and split black swallow-tailed ribbons hanging down the back. I asked him once how he spent the last day of the war. He told me that he had taken three of his best friends, a pack of cards, and a bottle of Johnny Walker down to the deepest dugout they could find and played bridge, their enjoyment spoilt only by an American Artillery battery up top trying to be the last one to fire a shot in the war.

He would also relate funny stories of that time, such as the pigeon officer who wrote on the message attached to the creature's leg and which arrived with much flutter at headquarters, with the words "I am fed up with carrying this fucking bird across France."

My grandfather once asked me, when I was staying with him, "What does your father do with his money?" He held in his hand a letter from Dad apparently asking for funds.

"I don't know sir," I said.

"Women?" he asked.

"No, I don't think so."

"Gambling?"

"No."

"Oh," he said exasperatingly, and wandered away, brows furrowed. Dear old thing. He didn't mention what I knew to be the real problem. Drink.

Granddad told me once of the mess my father had got into with money losses at cards during the war, and how he had asked for help, which had been withheld, forcing Dad to take extreme measures, which included selling his medals, borrowing, begging, but I don't think stealing, enough cash to get over to France where he worked on a lavender farm in Provence, stole the farmer's lorry and got to Marseilles, where he bluffed his way onto a tramp steamer as a deck hand and went with it to Egypt, where his brother had a job with an oil company and managed to get him a job as an accounting clerk. I believe he met my Italian mother in Cairo, then married and settled in Alexandria for a short time before returning to England.

My childhood memories begin about that time. It was a life full of moment and movement. We spent time in England, living mostly in hotels or with friends, and periods in the Middle East, both in Egypt and in what was then called Palestine. A British mandated territory at the time, as basically was Egypt. The Brits ran everything, and, considering the problems of the day, I think rather well.

In Palestine, times were especially hard with ambushes common, bombs going off all over the place, the Arabs in full revolt against British rule and the increasingly overwhelming influx of Jewish emigrants. The year would have been around 1936. We lived in Haifa in a new house half way up Mount Carmel. My sister and I, for some reason, were sent to a German school, where we and a few other English and American children were bullied unmercifully by the German kids. I was never sure why, there were so many German people there, but I know I didn't like them very much.

The times between were spent running around the

upper decks of various P&O and British India ships with names like Barradine, Barrallat, and Barraboole, playing hide and seek with other children going to Egypt or India or Australia...

⁂ ⁂ ⁂ ⁂

The ships left Tilbury in London, sailed uncomfortably through the channel and the Bay of Biscay, arriving in another world of smooth seas, blue waters, and Mediterranean lushness at Gibraltar before continuing on to Malta and Port Said where we got off.

The life in Egypt was mostly quite luxurious. We had a large house in a suburb of Alexandria called Zizinia. One didn't have to have a lot of money to afford servants. We had a cook, a maid, and a gardener. Madeleine and I shared an Armenian nanny, who, at one point let her lover into the house when Mum and Dad were at a party, so that he could burgle the house. Madeleine, who was all of eight at the time, managed to get to the phone and call the police, who came and caught the culprits red-handed. I got so excited I was sick all over one of the Arab policemen.

We used to be taken to the beach, which was close by, and would swim and play in the gentle creamy surf at lunchtime. We would eat a marvelous sandwich similar to a hamburger, but flatter, and made of an unleavened bread like pita, but tastier, with a highly spiced mince meat. We would drink a sweet fizzy concoction called Tizer and follow up with the best ice cream in the world, a chocolate tube with a stick for holding. The last part always fell off into the sand as it melted.

My sister Madeleine

When we moved to Palestine, Dad having transferred to another company, the same trips to the beach were less carefree. The Arab revolt was in full swing. All the sojourns were made in protected convoys and all the dads carried weapons. Cecil had his Webley revolver from the trenches, which Mum had smuggled through customs when we joined him. Nobody ever attacked us, but there was always tension about and many outrages were effected by both sides. Nothing much seems to have changed.

⁂ ⁂ ⁂ ⁂

The relationship with my father was from then, until after the war and into the fifties, intermittent, to say the least. Walking one evening down Bond Street on my way to a date, I noticed this very tall man coming towards me in the crowd. We passed, but I glanced back thinking, "Was it? Yes it was!"

He looked back too, a look of recognition. "Is it Teddy? ... My God, it's you."

We hadn't seen each other for at least two or three years. This was so, so strange. I went to give him a hug. That was a mistake. One doesn't hug my Dad, "People will think we're queer." He looked around embarrassedly. He looked at me. People swirled about us. "Would you like a drink?"

We went into a pub that happened to be right where we had been standing.

"So," said Dad "How are you?" Then without waiting for an answer, looked at the bartender and said "A pint of bitter for me," and looking rather doubtfully at me, said, "and I think a small light ale for you. Well how's your health?"

"Very well thank you," adding, "I've just been circumcised.

"Good God, are you going to Palestine?"

"No, it was something I had to have done," which, for certain anatomical reasons, was true.

"Oh well, is your work progressing well? You wouldn't have a cigarette would you? I seem to be out of them at the moment."

I offered him a Gold Flake.

"Oh thanks. Yes, hm, yes. All going well at my end. Yes swimmingly, I would say."

I looked at him. He looked a bit shabby. The suit was obviously a good one, but a bit worn and shiny at the elbows. 'Oh dear, I think Dad's not doing too well.' I wasn't surprised then when he said:

"Are you alright for funds?" Although in a tone of voice that affected concern for my welfare, he followed this sally with, "Couldn't let me have a fiver could you? Bit short I'm afraid."

I didn't have that much on me, but was able to find a pound that he gratefully accepted. We chatted briefly and then parted. He invited me to tea for the next week. I accepted and decided to take Hazel a Windmill Revue dancer, with me to meet Dad and Connie, my step-mama. We had a pleasant time, marred only, for me, with Dad trying to get off with Hazel, much to my discomfiture and Connie's distaste.

After tea we went to a little drinks club that Connie ran in Portman Square. It was typical of that type of establishment. It was a private, all-hours drinking club, in a basement, dark, cozy, and quiet. Connie went behind the bar to help serve the customers, all of whom she knew.

Cecil leaned against the bar and was soon surrounded by chums who encouraged him to tell stories. He launched into the battles of north and east Africa. He was a good storyteller and everyone in the circle was entranced. Drinks came thick and fast. I noticed he never bought a round. He had a habit of snuffling and pulling his moustache, especially when describing the juicy bits.

At one point Connie said, "For Christ's sake Cecil, stop shoving your moustache up your nose and buy another drink."

"Yes, yes," he said looking nervously at me. I pretended not to have heard.

Later Connie prevailed on me to come every Wednesday to dance with the single older ladies, a sort of polite gigolo. I got all my drinks and food free. It worked well, and I got several rather dubious offers. I declined them all.

Though our times together were comparatively infrequent, those that occurred were often amusing and informative. He filled my impressionable mind with all sorts of useless but whimsical items of Edwardian and Victorian England. Never carry an umbrella to the country, he would advise. Never run up to either a horse or a woman. Under no circumstances wear a russet suit to the city or wear a blue suit with brown shoes, to which he referred as the "Welsh national costume." Always know when to leave a party. And never complain and never explain.

He was very helpful in influencing my taste in literature and even wrote down a list of everything I should read, from A to Z. All the classics, poetry, fiction, historical works. "Read everything," he would say. "Learn, listen, be attentive, and don't talk too much." The last, I'm afraid, I tended to ignore, sometimes a mistake I think.

He introduced me to those marvelously funny English comedies of literature of the time. "The Autobiography of a Nobody." The works of Belloc and of Chesterton and Lear. He would recite bits of comic verse about young men who 'forgot to lock the bathroom door, allowing maiden aunts to walk in on their ablutions, slip on the soap, fall down and break their neck, and so, who, with one fell swoop and plunge lost his honour, his aunt, and his sponge.' Or the chap, who was having an affair with a doctor's wife, so ate an apple every day to keep that doctor far away.

My mother's influence on me was of a different complexion. She had a gentle, non-combative nature most of the time, though when roused by what she perceived as injustice or unfair play, she was like a tiger. She was wonderful to us and loved my father deeply, however badly he behaved. In spite of it all, she put up with all sorts of indignities and made a relatively happy home for us all, cheering us up when blue, and mending us when broken. Sadly, she was not herself strong, physically, and was subject to a variety of ills. The English climate didn't suit her and she missed her native Italy, its sunshine and gaiety, badly.

When the war came, and father left for his service, she had to deal with many different problems and complications like rationing, air raid precautions, looking after us, and working to put food on the table. She was a talented and sought-after dressmaker, slaving to meet deadlines and dealing with difficult customers.

Then the bombing began. Tragically the combination of all these tribulations led to further deterioration in her health, until she succumbed at the age of 39. We were plunged into hopeless grief. She was beloved by all who knew her and had been touched by her caring and compassionate nature. I have her to thank for the qualities she passed to me. My life would not have been so pleasant or agreeable without the precepts of good manners she taught me.

* * * *

My work continued to interest me and I had obtained a lot of new business for my company, so was making enough money to keep us in relative comfort. Vicky seemed to be doing well at school and had lots of friends who adored her.

Vianne had obtained a wonderful job at the Stratford Festival in the publicity department and seemed happy.

A shadow was however, lurking on the horizon. Inevitably, it seems, priorities become confused in marriages, especially as the first years pass and certain matters gain importance over others. Economic imponderables edge careless raptures to the sidelines. Problems of a domestic nature dominate; work and school responsibilities interfere with romantic ideals and sentimental emotions. Thus it was that one day, Vianne told me that she was leaving. I tried to tell myself that this would indeed be temporary, but knew in my heart that love had flown out of the window.

I'm sure Vicky sensed the worst too, but we all put the best face on things and carried on as normally as we could. Right up to Vianne getting on the airport bus, I couldn't quite believe what was happening. I was numb. This was too sad. Maybe she will come back I thought. I drove Vicky to school in silence, dropped her off, and went to work feeling depleted and empty.

The following days and weeks and months were awful. I missed Vianne dreadfully. I missed coming home to a house of laughter, argument, and family. The life domestic really had suited me, warts and all. Now the house was silent, lonely, and without charm. I looked ahead with foreboding.

Vicky and I struggled along, but this arrangement was not working. A second breakup had to happen, and it did, the whole depressing procedure as before, repeated, as I saw her off in the bus to the airport. The house was really unappealing that night and troubled dreams haunted me.

The house seemed more haunted now too. Sometimes I would be working in the front garden, which was large and extended down almost to the stream, when I would stop for a rest, and look up to the house across the lawn. The house would stare at me, its windows reflecting the images of life like those opaque sunglasses that people wear when you can't see their eyes, just your own face mirrored, grotesque, misshapen, and sinister. I really felt as though it resented my presence.

In an odd sort of way their absence reminded me of the time I gave up smoking though on a much, much greater scale. There was always the feeling that something important in one's life was missing.

* * * *

Thankfully matters improved. After a dreary couple of months I met new people and seemed to be having a more balanced life. The house was still too full of memories, and I did still keep expecting to see Vi or Vicky when I turned a corner or looked up at what sounded like a step or a voice, both turning out to be the wood creaking or the wind howling dolefully through the trees.

Then, one day, walking idly through the grocery store in Stratford, trying to remember what Vianne used to feed me, and never remembering, and finishing up buying cold ham and the makings of a salad and a few spuds, I saw this young woman, tall, graceful, and quite beautiful, hair luxuriant, Titian, billowing down to her waist. She looked like a Rossetti model.

She was dressed in the most attractive outdoorsy way, heavy, white, fisherman's polo neck sweater, hip-length sheepskin coat, open, jeans tucked into green Wellies. The first thing I thought was that I wanted an outfit just like it. Then I sidled up and tried to catch the eye. No success. I looped around the aisles trying to put myself in her path so that there could be an 'accidental' encounter.

"Damn! Here comes what's-his-name, the bore of the town, chatter, chatter, chatter." I felt like telling him to bugger off, but restrained myself. In a way this worked in my favour, as I saw her look up when I spoke. A brief flicker of interest, then she was gone.

"Blast and sod it." She was too far ahead in the line-up at checkout and by the time I got to the parking lot she was gone.

This is when I believe that there is some sort of plan to life. That it isn't just luck and accident. I'm driving down Waterloo Street, when I see the bright auburn hair and the bobbing, undulating, sexy walk. She has a little boy with her. I determine to follow and turn the car up Cobourg Street. The wrong way up a one-way road.

'Oh well. This is too important to worry about such niceties.' I slowed and rolled the window down.

"Hello," I said.

"Hi." She smiled.

That's something.

"I wanted to talk to you the other day in Loblaws."

"Yes, I know."

I was now stopped and parked, though still facing the wrong way. She was even more lovely than I had thought before, with eyes that were large and well-shaped, clear, and lustrous, skin that only red-heads have, ivory, peerless and transparent, a wonderful mouth, full, generous and mobile.

'Oh she was gorgeous.' We talked. She was a Brit too. The electricity was immediate. I drove away on top of the world. We were to meet again.

* * * *

It was spring, just the right time. She came out to the farm for tea. She stayed for drinks. I felt quite reckless and very young. She made me feel attractive and I loved her for it.

The next time I saw her, she surprised me by coming out to the farm on her bicycle. I got home from work to see this strange bike on my lawn and on entering the house was greeted by a lovely aroma of roasting lamb. She had prepared a dinner of rack of lamb with new potatoes, peas, and mint sauce, followed by a glowing steaming treacle tart with custard. A gin and tonic was pressed into my hand and I was bidden to relax. Needless to say I was captured. That night she stayed, and from then on life took on a complete new meaning.

I met her mum and dad who were wonderful Brits of the old school, with good manners and a strong sense of what was proper and what was not. Mary also had two marvelous children, a boy and a girl, eight and six. We took to each other at once and were to have some great times chasing around the farm playing games and having parties. It was a magic time in my life and it was as if I was being given another chance of family life. I embraced it with enthusiasm.

❋ ❋ ❋ ❋

In a little while we decided that Mary should come to live with me, which led to another chapter, that of playing squire and chatelaine. We gave terrific parties and got to know more and more people. All the old crowd from my previous marriage were still close, and all adored Mary, and now we had new chums from Mary's world, many of them backstage workers from the Festival Theatre. Mary was, at this time, a dresser at the theatre.

It was fun to see the world's mix, that of the business man, farmer, doctor, and lawyer, mostly established and successful, and if not square, certainly very straight, with that of the theatre, young, versatile, reckless, and usually perfumed with musk and marijuana, an oddly attractive and dangerously seductive combination.

❋ ❋ ❋ ❋

It was now the late eighties. We decided to marry, and to marry well, we wanted church bells and big hats, pipers and confetti. The reception was to be held at the farm and we were blessed with a sparkling summer day.

The wedding ceremony went well after the lovable local minister agreed to go through the ritual in spite of the fact that I'd forgotten to get a license. We were formally married the following week at the City Hall in Stratford.

The reception was splendid. Everyone got drunk, including the two pipers who kept marching up and down long after most of the guests had either left or were sleeping somewhere in the house.

Cutting the cake with Paddy Crean's Sword

Mary and I escaped to Bayfield and spent a sleepless night next to a couple who quarreled loudly and without end all night.

Vicky and I at my wedding. Hookway farm

We returned to the farm a few days later and got on with the things that one does. Mary was working at an art framing shop and I was getting busier and busier at my job. In between we loved and played and generally had a life that was quite peerless.

Some say, "Be careful what you wish for." The Chinese say "May you live in interesting times," and they don't mean it in a pleasant way. Some think that if things are going too well, something awful is around the corner. So it was with us, or rather with me. Shadows were gathering that would almost overwhelm me.

❋ ❋ ❋ ❋

We had gone to England that hot summer of 1990. I had noticed that my energy level was low and that I was tired all the time. I felt lackluster and irritable. We went and watched the Queen Mother's 90th birthday parade at the Horse Guards. It was a grand affair and especially exciting watching it from my cousin's office window in the old Admiralty Office, which was now being used by the Northern Irish Office, a department for which John was Deputy Secretary of State.

I wasn't feeling too bad that day, probably because I was full of good champagne that was lavishly provided. At one point during a break in the proceedings, John said to me, "You were a sailor weren't you Teddy?"

I said "Yes."

"Would you like to see Winnie's old office?"

"I certainly would," said I.

"Follow me," said he. We went down endless corridors, turned corners, climbed stairs, opened and closed numerous doors, and finally came to an office in which sat four or five elderly women sitting at typewriters. They looked up. One said, "Good afternoon Minister."

"Oh Edith, could I have the keys? I'd like my cousin here from Canada to see his office."

"Of course sir." She produced some heavy-looking old keys and handed them to John. He went over to a large door and opened it. It was dark inside. He turned on the light. Facing me was a large desk behind which was a wide curtained floor-to-ceiling window, leather chairs, small tables with lamps, bookcases tightly packed with books of all description, on one wall an enormous map of the world.

I stood transfixed. This was where Winston Churchill had directed the British Fleets in both World Wars. This was where Gallipoli was planned. My thoughts were interrupted by John saying, "This was where Able Seaman Teddy Payne got his orders." Surreal is the word for the way I felt. We went back to the others and went on watching the panoply and circumstance of the remainder of the celebrations.

When it was all over we went down to the car and waited, while John's chauffeuse checked for explosive devices under the chassis using a mirror on a long pole. John's Irish duties made him and his family particularly subject to terrorist attention. We went on to a restaurant and dined with all the family.

All the time I kept thinking, 'Why aren't I enjoying this as much as I should be?' I felt strangely distanced from everyone, had a searing headache and just wanted to go to bed. The evening was finally over and we took the tube home.

In the past I had always hated leaving England as the times there had inevitably been enjoyable. This time I couldn't wait to get home and, I suppose, see my doctor. I wasn't sure what I would do. Sometimes my head wouldn't ache and my sleeping seemed better but the tiredness and ennui continued. I worried.

My doctor told me that he could find nothing wrong, and that on the face of it, I was probably just stressed, and gave me the usual pill and advice to go home and stop worrying. I was relieved, but couldn't get rid of the nagging feeling that something was amiss.

Then came another blow. The furniture business in Canada was dying. The division of the paint company that I ran was being closed down and my job with it. I could scarcely believe this misfortune. I went home to tell Mary, who was aghast. She, being the sensible girl she was, came hastily to the conclusion that we had to quickly make plans for retrenchment and the first thing we had to sell was the farm. That night the brief snatches of sleep were abrim with nightmares.

My life then descended into a blurred, dark, strange place. Sleep completely abandoned me. I tried even reading Hardy or at least some of his more complicated passages. Pills didn't work, and the headaches grew worse. I had difficulty walking, dragging a leg. They thought I'd had a stroke but were wrong. Finally Mary insisted on hospital care and off to London I went. There, X-rays were followed by MRIs. I was medicated up to the hilt and felt like death warmed up.

One morning I was perambulating gently down a corridor dragging one foot and a portable gizmo that was holding the mixture being injected into my bloodstream, when one of the doctors on the team working on me approached. He remarked, rather too cheerfully I thought, "We know what's wrong with you. You've got a brain tumor."

So that's it, I thought. It's all over. I tried to listen to what this man was saying, but felt so overwhelmed that all I could hear was a jumble of sounds that meant nothing. He helped me back to my room, and with a nurse's assistance, put me to bed. I lay back and tried not to think. They gave me another pill to make me sleep and I faded into blessed oblivion.

I woke after a wonderful sleep filled with marvelous dreams about how well I was and how happy life around me was. Reality came with a shock. A blast of bitter remorse and deep depression. Breakfast came and went, kind nurses applied themselves to my toilet and puffed up the pillow. The door opened and in came the team headed by a tall, distinguished man with the face of a middle-aged angel. This turned out to be one of the most brilliant neurosurgeons of the day.

He explained that what I had was called a

meninginoma and that he was sure it could be removed and, oh joy of joys, it wasn't nasty, it was benign. Immediate surgery was however imperative. That I wanted to embrace this man and cover him with kisses doesn't begin to describe how I felt. Mary arrived soon after and we wept together with relief.

The operation lasted seven hours, and when I woke up, Mary was by my side, wiping blood off my shaven head and welcoming me back to a headache-free world. Her lovely face smiling softly at me was the first thing I saw, and thought, "Heaven, that's where I am."

Rest and recuperation followed, then home to a new house. While I was conveniently in hospital, poor Mary had sold the farm and had moved to a new place in Stratford. In my illness I'd forgotten even that we had looked at houses together and had picked a darling little Ontario cottage.

Strange, an entire two weeks of my life were gone. No memories at all. So many things had happened in such a short time, and yet a blank wall met all efforts to recall. Though I felt better physically, mentally it had all been too much and a downfall was on the way. Dark clouds had not gone entirely away. More tribulations were to follow.

Superstitions have played a part in my life. My mother, a central Italian, had been very aware of otherworldly things. Manifestations of the spirit world were important and not to be mocked. She would pick up a crust of bread dropped on the floor and kiss it, making reference to the body of Christ. Salt spilt would be flung over the right shoulder. There was a fish, what was it, a haddock or a plaice, I can't remember, but it had what looked like a human thumbprint on its flank. This was the mark of God's hand when handing out the loaves and fishes.

All this and more followed me through life. "Don't be too full of yourself," she warned me, when matters were going too well. "Watch out for the inevitable trip over the carpet-edge of life." So it was that I remonstrated with myself on my present misfortunes. Things had been going too swimmingly. It was time for the crash.

The depression from before the operation returned, this time so extreme I could not raise my head to look about, couldn't speak, wanted to die. It was the most catastrophic time of my life. Mary, really alarmed, called the ambulance, and I was whisked off to emergency. After the usual wait, I was interviewed, and when they realized I was suicidal, they looked at each other meaningfully and carted me off to a ward known locally as 2 South.

At the time I didn't realize what this meant, but felt uneasy when the door of the ward closed behind me with a heavy thump and locked. Now, with stomach well into my boots, I looked about me. It was a large room that seemed like an entrance hall leading to a bigger ward beyond. It was in the first room that I was questioned.

When they discovered that I had just had a serious

brain operation they went into action. Although at the time I had no idea what was happening, I was subsequently to learn that they put me on a program of tranquillizers and a diet of liquids and foods and medications to clear me of all the drugs with which my body was still full from the surgery.

It took about two weeks to put things to right. The transformation was painful, and I had some frightening nights, but the care given was copious and skilful and recovery finally occurred.

I have to record that part of the curing process came about when I considered my fellow patients and realized that my problem could be solved and that what I was going through was transitory. Most of these people were seriously ill and their salvation was not to be so easily vouchsafed.

Many of these unhappy individuals were women, some with self-inflicted wounds. Wrists that were bandaged were a not uncommon sight. Some weren't mentally unstable, but depressed. Some were wives of farmers and had had to help with the chores, look after children, and work a second job as house cleaners. They were basically exhausted, mentally and physically. I noticed the husbands never came to visit, leading me to suspect that love was absent too. Sad. I would listen to their woeful tales hour after hour. All they wanted was to talk and have someone listen. I was glad to fill this role. It seemed the least I could do.

One glorious morning I awoke feeling that all clouds were lifted. I felt cleaned out. My mind was clear and untroubled, my body felt strong and sturdy. I checked at the desk and was greeted with smiles and conviviality. Mary was sent for, and I was allowed to go home for the weekend. The joy of being outdoors again, to see and hear and smell all the simple things we all take so much for granted, was almost too much to bear. I wanted to laugh and cry at the same time.

The experiences I had been through, though alarming, unpleasant, and sometimes terrifying, were salutary in the sense that I stopped worrying about things that had seemed so important before. Minor irritations ceased to bother me as they had in the past. I stopped getting my knickers in a twist, as Mary used to put it. Life took on a much rosier hue. I had looked mortality in the eye and survived. For this and other blessings I am truly thankful.

Now, I'm surrounded with affection and close friends. As someone once said, "When all is said and done, all that matters in the end is the laughter and love of good friends."

··· *end* ···

Postscript

In the cinema, sometimes facts are changed; sometimes there is exaggeration, often elaboration, and commonly gross untruths. Thus my initial expectations of America were quite erroneous. So, while I was led to believe it would be all fun and games, I wasn't prepared for the gritty, grey banality and indifference of the mid-west in winter where everyone seemed to go to church on Sundays and boredom yawned in my face. But, I grew and learned and stretched.

I adjusted as I went along, and did, now and again, find the America I had expected. Most people were excessively kind to me, helpful, thoughtful, and generous and I have never regretted going there. I did fall in love with a wonderful woman and with her, had a marvelous daughter. I worked and played there and had experiences that could not have happened anywhere else. Overall, I had an enormously good time.

Moving to Canada was a big step but, again, one which I think was wise. I fell in love again there. Canada, I tell my American friends, is like America would have been had we not had that unfortunate misunderstanding in 1776. Canada has the love of law and order, the reticence, and the respect for privacy that the Brits embrace, combined with a certain pioneer open-handedness of the Americans, an attitude of frank dealing unencumbered by too many bits of traditional furniture. It's a great combination. I do also prefer the monarchical system, so that was an added attraction.

I am convinced that I would rather be lucky than clever, and that's basically the gift that I have been given. My father was very clever, but terribly unlucky: never at the right place at the right time, a cloud seemed to follow him around. I, on the other hand, was never very smart, but constantly blessed with the cards being dealt in my favour. For that, I shall be eternally grateful.

Biography

Edward Payne's roots are in Constable country, the counties of Suffolk and Norfolk in Eastern England. He completed his formal art education in Norwich and London. These beginnings have had a huge influence on the way he sees and writes about life. Although not really dwelt on in his story here, it should be noted that Teddy has also become an accomplished watercolour artist along the way.

"Throughout my life the facility I had to draw and paint has been a great source of pleasure, comfort, and more latterly profit. I have been able to make a modest living from producing small watercolours of a variety of subjects ranging from simple landscapes and townscapes through decorative interiors, to quite complex studies of marine and aviation subjects. I can't remember exactly when I discovered I could draw, but I must have been very young. My father could draw quite well and probably instilled an interest in me in the subject. Inevitably and concurrently I learnt to appreciate all forms of art and art history, becoming, I think, more perceptive to all about me and more aware of the general and specific aspects of life, natural and organic, as well as mechanical, architectural, and technical."

Teddy currently lives in Stratford, Ontario, where he continues to pursue his work as a watercolour artist, along with his writing, reading, and gardening.